How to Talk with Families About Genetics and Psychiatric Illness

How to Talk with Families About Genetics and Psychiatric Illness

Holly Peay
Jehannine Austin

W. W. Norton & Company
New York • London

Jar model illustrations reproduced by permission of Cindy Campbell-Lashley

For information about permission to reproduce selections from this book, write to
Permissions, W. W. Norton & Company, Inc., 500 Fifth Avenue, New York, NY 10110

For information about special discounts for bulk purchases, please contact
W. W. Norton Special Sales at specialsales@wwnorton.com or 800-233-4830

Manufacturing by Malloy Printing
Production manager: Leeann Graham

Library of Congress Cataloging-in-Publication Data

Peay, Holly.
  How to talk with families about genetics and psychiatric illness / Holly Peay,
Jehannine Austin. — 1st ed.
       p. ; cm.
  "A Norton professional book."
  Includes bibliographical references and index.
  ISBN 978-0-393-70549-2 (pbk.)
  1. Mental illness—Genetic aspects.   2. Family counseling.   3. Linkage (Genetics)
4. Family counseling—Genetics.   I. Austin, Jehannine.   II. Title.
  [DNLM: 1. Mental Disorders—genetics.   2. Family Relations.   3. Genetic
Counseling—methods.   4. Medical History Taking.   WM 140]
  RC455.4.G4P43 2011
  616.89'042—dc22   2010034793

ISBN: 978-0-393-70549-2 (pbk.)

W. W. Norton & Company, Inc., 500 Fifth Avenue, New York, N.Y. 10110
www.wwnorton.com
W. W. Norton & Company Ltd., Castle House, 75/76 Wells Street, London W1T 3QT

1 2 3 4 5 6 7 8 9 0

Contents

Acknowledgments

During the writing of this book, I was supported by the Canadian Institutes of Health Research, the Michael Smith Foundation for Health Research, and the Provincial Health Services Authority of British Columbia.

I would like to gratefully acknowledge the mentorship of Dr. W.G. Honer, and the support of my fantastic research team without whom it would have been impossible to devote the time necessary to complete this project. Special thanks go to Catriona Hippman, Angela Inglis, Andrea Ringrose, and Emily Morris.

I would also like to thank all the individuals who have mental illness and their family members with whom I have had the privilege of interacting, and from whom I have learned so much about how to talk to families about genetics and mental illness.

Thanks to Claudea for the "mental illness jars" artwork that we use in Chapter 4! Thanks too to Erin Michalak for bravely rescuing me from a black bear that terrified me in the middle of the night while I was on a retreat, writing this book!

Last, but most of all, this book would not have been possible without the support and encouragement of my family: Sonia, my brother Ben, and my parents Chris and Hedley. Thank you!

—Jehannine Austin

During a period of the writing of this book, I was supported by the intramural program of the National Human Genome Research Institute of the National Institutes of Health. I greatly appreciate the support and tolerance of my husband, Clint Peay, and my children Miles, Alec, and Simone. Joseph McInerney and Barbara Biesecker have been, and continue to be, inspirational mentors. Finally, my deepest appreciation goes to the clients and research participants who have shared their stories with me.

—Holly Peay

Preface

Your client asks you, "Why did I get this psychiatric illness?"
Your client's sibling asks you, "Will it happen to me, too?"
What if you could answer these questions in a meaningful way?
Imagine the effect on your clients, their families, and on public health. Consider the emotional, economic, and ethical implications in your practice and in society. As we continue to gain knowledge related to the causes of psychiatric illness, we are better able to answer these questions for clients and their relatives.

Clients' first question about the cause of their illness—"Why did I get this psychiatric illness?"—is often accompanied by a second: "Does this mean that other people in my family are more likely to develop this illness?" This question is usually associated with considerable fear—so much so, in fact, that healthy relatives of individuals with psychiatric illness frequently overestimate the chance of other family members becoming ill, and may decide not to have families of their own as a result of the fear that their children might develop one of these devastating illnesses (Austin, Smith & Honer, 2006).

The purpose of this book is to provide you, the mental health clinician, with tools to address spoken or unspoken questions about why and how the illness developed and about risks of other family members becoming affected. This book will also help you identify clients who would benefit from a referral for a consultation with a genetics professional. We have focused this book on major psychiatric illnesses that typically arise during adolescence or young adulthood, including bipolar disorder, schizoaffective disorder, and schizophrenia. We chose this focus because, compared to other psychiatric illnesses, more is known about the causes of and risks for these disorders, and they represent the area in which we (the authors) have the most experience. The general concepts in this book, however, can be applied just as easily to other mood and psychotic disorders as well as other disorders such as autism, attention-deficit/hyperactivity disorder, alcoholism, eating disorders, obsessive–compulsive disorder, and Tourette syndrome.

We appreciate that many mental health clinicians have limited interactions with unaffected relatives of clients, and that the interactions that do occur may be confined to specific topics. However, because issues around the causes of psychiatric illnesses and the risks to unaffected family members are so pertinent to relatives of affected individuals, we highlight them and encourage clinicians to engage close relatives in discussions of cause and risk whenever possible.

A Few Caveats to Consider

Over recent decades, research efforts aimed at discovering the factors that contribute to the development of a psychiatric illness have been intense. This research has generated a broad and generally agreed-upon understanding of the causes of psychiatric illness. However, though researchers are confident about understanding the causes of psychiatric illness in broad, general terms, it currently remains impossible to determine for any one affected individual exactly which specific factors contributed to his or her particular illness. While we cannot yet *definitively* answer questions about the specific causes and risks for any one client with psychiatric illness, we can use research data together with the individual's personal and family psychiatric history to provide information about likely causes of his or her illness and about the magnitude of risk for family members.

This book will not prepare you to provide genetic counseling services in the same way that such services would be provided by an individual with specialized training. Neither will this book equip you with all of the skills and tools necessary to meet all the needs of every family. Some individuals will still require and benefit from the specialist services provided by a referral to a genetics professional.

This book will assist you in helping families deal with common psychiatric illnesses that are unrelated to the presence of a genetic syndrome; we provide only very limited information about genetic syndromes that include psychiatric features as one of the manifestations. Although a number of genetic syndromes are associated with psychiatric disorders (e.g., Rett syndrome, 22q11 deletion syndrome, Prader–Willi syndrome, fragile X syndrome), the proportion of all cases of psychiatric illness that are associated with a genetic syndrome is very small.

A Word about Genetic Counseling

Genetic counseling is a term that first appeared in the 1940s, when it was defined by Sheldon Reed as a "kind of genetic social-work without eugenic connotations" (Reed, 1975, p. 335). Genetic counseling is often incorrectly viewed as being relevant only in the context of pregnancy (e.g., talking about the chance of an unborn child having Down syndrome) or in situations where a family member has a (relatively) rare genetic disorder, such as cystic fibrosis or sickle cell disease. Although genetic counseling is certainly well suited to these situations, there is a far broader range of circumstances in which it can be usefully employed.

In fact, *genetic counseling* can be applied to all conditions that have a genetic component. It includes the process of addressing concerns about the causes of an illness and about the risks of it occurring in the family members of an affected individual (Resta, 2006; Resta et al., 2006). When framed this way, it is easy to see its relevance to psychiatric illnesses. And contrary to the implication inherent in its name, genetic counseling is not limited to addressing only *genetic* contributions to illnesses. Rather, this form of counseling includes discussing all known contributors to disease pathogenesis in a holistic manner. Despite the applicability of genetic counseling to psychiatric illnesses, there is an insufficient number of specifically trained professionals to meet the needs of the individuals with psychiatric illness and their family members who might benefit from this intervention. The large majority of this population never has access to a genetics professional (Hunter, 2010).

Questions such as "Why did I get this illness?" and "Does this mean that there are increased risks for my family members, too?" are so fundamental that all mental health clinicians are faced with having to respond to them. Clinicians need to be able to provide accurate, understandable explanations about the causes of psychiatric illness and information about familial risks. In many regards, mental health clinicians are ideally placed to provide this kind of education and counseling, as they often acquire knowledge of their clients' needs and family histories in the context of their ongoing therapeutic relationships. Many clients will feel more comfortable discussing these issues with a known clinician within a supportive, ongoing relationship. However, research has shown that many mental health clinicians feel inadequately prepared to address questions about these topics (Finn et al., 2005).

The time is ripe for clinicians to integrate education and counseling about genetically related causes and family-centered risk factors into their mental health practices. Research findings support the value of providing such information to clients, and clients increasingly demand such information from their clinicians. We provide advice in this book that allows clinicians to begin these important conversations. We base our advice on our experiences with providing genetic counseling to families and affected individuals, our research experience in the same area, and our knowledge of the relevant research literature. We hope that this book will be a useful guide that allows you to expand and deepen your knowledge about the causes of psychiatric illnesses, familial risk factors, and the significance of these issues for affected individuals and their family members.

How to Talk with Families About Genetics and Psychiatric Illness

Introduction

Understanding Genetic Counseling in Relation to Psychiatric Illness

Strong scientific data support the assertion that major psychiatric illnesses, including psychotic disorders, mood disorders, anxiety disorders, and autistic spectrum disorders, are typically caused by the combined influences of both genetic and environmental factors (Finn & Smoller, 2006). Research data allow us to provide clients with more information about these contributing factors. It is important that when interpreting and applying such data for clients, we keep in mind the ethical, legal, and social implications of the information and services we provide.

Guiding Ethos of Genetics Counseling

Discussions about the causes of psychiatric illness and the risks to other family members of becoming affected are deeply personal and may involve existential questions from clients and their relatives. In particular, decision-making about family planning and risk-reduction strategies can hinge on very personal perceptions of illness severity and burden, as well as the perception of the actual numerical probability that an individual may be affected.

Although clients may look to you for advice, we encourage you to maintain a client-centered ethos. Client-centered counseling is a Rogerian approach in which clinicians encourage clients to share information and express feelings. Clinicians do not suggest how clients should perceive information about cause or risk, make decisions, or make life plans. Instead, by listening and mirroring back what clients reveal, clinicians help them explore and understand their perceptions of family and personal risk. Clinicians facilitate decision-making and life planning by helping clients integrate the information provided into their perceptions about psychiatric illness. Your existing therapeutic relationship with your clients will allow you to help them make decisions or life plans that are consistent with the values and beliefs that have meaning for them.

This client-centered approach has been termed *nondirective* and unfortunately, this concept is sometimes misinterpreted as requiring the clinician to simply deflect any requests for advice (Weil, 2003). For example, the following response to a common request for guidance illustrates a nondirective approach that is unlikely to be effective.

> *Question*: "I just can't decide what's right. I really want a child, but I'm so afraid it will end up having the same problems I have. What should I do?"
>
> *Response*: "It's a difficult situation, but I wouldn't feel right telling you what to do." Or, "I have never been in your situation, and I can't possibly understand what it feels like. Whatever you choose will be right for you."

A more constructive, client-centered response would be an empathic reflection, such as:

> *Response*: "You have talked for the past few months about your strong desire to have a child. But you've also told me how scary it seems. Overall, based on what you've told me, it seems to me that

you are leaning toward [having a baby/not having a baby]. Does that seem right? Let's talk more about where your fears come from, then, and see if I can help you work through the fears and clarify a decision that you will find satisfying."

Guiding Principles of Genetic Counseling

The ethical principles that provide the foundation for genetic counseling interactions are familiar to all clinicians. In some important ways, however, discussions about familial disorders (whether genetic or environmental, or a combination of both) may intensify the need to address and adhere to the principles.

- *Client autonomy and informed decisions.* Discussions about cause of illness and risk of other family members becoming affected require close attention to the maintenance of autonomy. These discussions can support autonomy by helping clients and relatives make meaning, cope and adapt, and make life plans that are informed by the most up-to-date information. Directive interactions in which the clinician tells the client what he or she should do, or interactions in which the clinician chooses not to share important information about cause or family risk, impinge upon the client's autonomy.

  An important way to protect your clients' autonomy is to carefully assess what they hope to learn about the causes of and risks for psychiatric illness. For example, some clients may seek the most specific quantitative assessment of risk possible (e.g., "There is about a 10% risk for the disorder to happen in a child"), whereas others prefer a qualitative assessment of risk (e.g., "This person's chance of becoming ill with the disorder is higher than for someone with no affected family members"). Others have no interest in risk assessment at all, but instead have questions about identification of early symptoms and early intervention. To allow for this variability, you might consider asking your clients what they want to learn at the beginning of discussions about causes of psychiatric illness and risk, and check in with them frequently to ensure that their needs are being met.

In some circumstances, it may be especially challenging to protect your clients' autonomy around issues of reproduction, as described in Chapter 7. The fact that risk for psychiatric disorders "runs in families," combined with clinicians' beliefs (which may be strongly held) about the ability of individuals with major psychiatric disorders to be effective parents, may lead to situations in which clinicians find it difficult to maintain a focus on client autonomy. In the near future, with the advent of genetic testing for susceptibility to psychiatric illness (as discussed in Chapter 13), maintaining autonomy may become more challenging. Already, direct-to-consumer companies are offering genetic testing for predisposition to psychiatric disorders and for specific personality traits, though the clinical utility of such genetic tests is extremely limited. Access to genetic testing is likely to continue to expand, and the clinical utility is likely to improve as our understanding of factors that contribute to psychiatric illness improves. Such testing will challenge what is required for informed consent. How you can work with your clients to help them understand more about genetic susceptibility testing is detailed in Chapter 11.

- *Beneficence and nonmaleficence.* When you engage in discussions around causes of psychiatric illness and the risk of family members becoming affected, it is not always clear how the information you provide will affect any individual client. This is because clients' perceptions of illness and risk, as well as their desired type and amount of information, vary considerably. Even in the case of predictive genetic testing for genes associated with considerable risk, receiving a positive test result has not been shown to cause long-term adverse outcomes for the majority of individuals (Marteau, 1998). In fact, individuals who choose such testing may use the process and the test results as part of the meaning-making and coping process. It will often be helpful to explore perceived benefits and harms with clients throughout the education and counseling process.

You may be concerned that information about risks for other family members to be affected could be harmful or shocking for your clients, and that entering into discussions about this may interfere with your therapeutic relationship. Our experience, supported by published research, suggests that many people with psychiatric illnesses and their relatives innately perceive that there is some level of increased risk for offspring to also have a psychiatric illness (Austin, Smith, & Honer, 2006; Peay et al., 2009). Most clients will not be harmed by an appropriately tailored, client-centered discussion about causes of illness and risks for illness recurrence in the family. If you have the benefit of an ongoing relationship with a client, you can carefully consider the timing and approach to these discussions. We have found that clinicians' ambivalence about such discussions often stems from concerns about their own knowledge base, their incomplete understanding of the causes of psychiatric illness, and their inability to prevent onset in at-risk individuals. Self-education and appropriate referrals may help clinicians feel more comfortable about their ability to support the principles of autonomy and beneficence when discussing causes of psychiatric illness and risks for family members.

At present there is no genetic testing for psychiatric illness that is of sufficient clinical utility to warrant widespread use (Mitchell et al., 2010), so genetic discrimination against at-risk individuals based on genetic test results is not yet of concern. Close relatives of individuals with psychiatric disorders may still face discrimination, however, in the form of a phenomenon known as "courtesy stigma," which may arise because of the importance of family history as a predictor for major psychiatric illness (Angermeyer et al., 2003; Corcoran et al., 2005). Indeed, depending on the psychiatric illness in the family, relatives are at increased risk for a range of psychiatric symptoms and disorders. Given this reality, maintaining an atmosphere of beneficence would be more straightforward if effective preventive measures were available to significantly reduce risk for these at-risk individuals. While this level of prevention is not yet possible, some interventions to decrease risk have been suggested (Amminger et al., 2010; see Chapter 8). Clinicians also can help clients manage uncertainty about risk to relatives, recognize early symptoms, and seek appropriate early interventions for at-risk individuals.

The Family as the Client

Discussions about cause of psychiatric illness and risks for family members may call into question the usually clear-cut delineation of "who is the client?" Genetic information is, by definition, family information, and risk information has relevance for at least all first-degree relatives (i.e., parents, siblings, and children) of an affected individual. Applying the concept of the "family as client" in mental health care may include, for example, helping clients with children understand how to identify and respond to early symptoms (should they emerge) in their children. More generally, you might want to raise the issue of sharing information about risk with relevant at-risk relatives. Though this type of discussion may involve an expansion of the traditional role of mental health clinicians, nonetheless it should be considered, as relatives may benefit from a consultation about causes of psychiatric illness and risk, especially after hearing about it from their affected relative. In the United States, clinicians may find it challenging to qualify for third-party reimbursement for consultation with healthy, at-risk individuals. Referral for genetic counseling for such individuals is appropriate.

Expanding Your Practice to Meet an Important but Neglected Need

Like many other mental health clinicians, you may be thinking, *"I am a busy clinician! Why should I make it a priority to discuss the causes of psychiatric illness and the risks for other family members with my clients?"* We would like to suggest a number of reasons.

- *Perception of cause of illness is important to how clients cope and adapt.*

As you know, psychiatric illnesses typically affect virtually every aspect of a person's life, and successfully adapting to them is extremely challenging. This challenge is even more significant because psychiatric illnesses are among the most profoundly stigmatized of all health conditions. Affected individuals and their family members typically react to the symptoms or diagnosis with anger, denial, hopelessness, guilt, and shame. Invariably, whether verbalized or not, this reaction is either followed or accompanied by an urgent need to understand why the disorder occurred. Indeed, the answer to the emotionally loaded question, *"Why did I get this psychiatric illness?"* may be critical to the client's interpretation of the meaning of the event and to the development of a much-needed sense of control over the illness. We know that when *not* provided with a comprehensive explanation for cause of illness, affected individuals and their families develop their own stories, based on their lived experiences and information they have gathered, to explain why the illness happened (Skirton, 2003). They are more likely to be uncertain about or to have incorrect or even damaging beliefs about the causes of their illness. For example, guilt about cause is common for affected individuals ("It's my own fault that I have this illness. If I hadn't done . . . then I wouldn't be ill now"). It is easy to see how such self-generated explanations for illness can be harmful to coping and adaptation, particularly if they invoke feelings of blame or guilt.

There is evidence that perceptions of cause of illness affect treatment adherence and help-seeking behaviors (Phelan, 2006). Specifically, if an affected individual blames him- or herself for causing the illness—attributing it to poor life decisions, lack of coping skills, or weak character, for example—then it makes sense that biological treatments such as medications are more likely to be rejected or not taken appropriately. Conversely, if an affected individual attributes his or her illness exclusively to biological factors, then psychological treatments, such as talking therapy, are likely to be rejected.

Understanding the causes of an illness is also useful to family members and partners/spouses of the affected individual. For example, parents of young people with severe mental illness often feel guilt about the cause of illness ("What did I do that caused this to happen to my son/daughter?"), and may even hazily recall having heard that psychiatric illness is caused by dysfunctional mother–child interaction (the "schizophrenogenic mother"). The support and involvement of family members may be positively affected by an accurate understanding of why the disorder occurred.

The reality is that all of your clients and their families are likely to have some kind of explanation for why their illness occurred, and almost all would benefit from a careful discussion in this area. The opportunity for your clients and their families to learn about and discuss the causes of psychiatric illness with you provides the potential to expose and address misconceptions that invoke stigma, shame, and other counteradaptive processes. Even if a client and his or her family has a sound understanding of the cause of illness, they may not feel confident that what they understand really applies to them personally. Even for your clients/families whose understanding is relatively clear and correct, it can be very empowering for such individuals if you confirm that their understanding is correct.

• *Education about causes of psychiatric illness is not comprehensively addressed elsewhere.*

Many clients rely on psychiatric advocacy organizations for detailed information about the causes of the disorder. Though such organizations often address cause of illness, many use a "chemical imbalance in the brain" explanation. This description may be useful for combating stigma, but it only goes part of the way to providing a complete explanation for many families, who then ask, "So what then causes the chemicals in the brain to become imbalanced?" A more comprehensive understanding of cause of illness is required in order to generate that much-needed sense of control over the illness.

Some clients may have the benefit of participating in psychoeducation programs related to their illness, but education about cause is typically not a primary focus of these programs. When cause of illness is addressed in psychoeducation, it is typically done in a group setting, in which only generalized messages can be provided about genes and environment working together to contribute to illness. As we describe in the following chapters, clients often hear these generalized messages but do not apply them to themselves. Personalizing the information about cause of illness by documenting a detailed psychiatric family history (as described in Chapter 3) and using it as an individualized educational tool can have a profound impact even for clients who are aware that, in general terms, genes and environment both contribute to the development of illness.

Anecdotally, many of our clients and their families have told us that they feel that no one wants to undertake a detailed discussion about illness cause or talk to them about issues of family recurrence. They therefore often feel isolated in regard to this important area. Broaching these difficult topics could lead to greater trust and better relationships with your clients and their families.

• *Family history is the most significant known risk factor for psychiatric illness.*

Having one first-degree relative with a major psychiatric disorder is the largest known risk factor for disorder onset in asymptomatic individuals. In other words, your client's children, siblings, and parents are (empirically) already in the highest known risk category for illness onset that is possible for asymptomatic individuals. That risk can increase even more if the family includes additional affected relatives and relatives with early ages at disorder onset, as described in Chapter 5.

- *Perceptions of risk may influence life planning, parenting, and decisions about childbearing.*

Just as affected individuals and families often have explanations regarding why the illness arose, it is also not unusual for them to have developed their own ideas about their own (or other family members') risk status for developing psychiatric illness. These ideas about who is at risk and how much risk exists may be based on perceptions of causes of illness, similarities to or differences from affected relatives, or on family or cultural beliefs. These existing impressions of risk status may or may not be accurate but can, in either case, have a dramatic impact on life planning. Large proportions of individuals with psychiatric illnesses and their families tend to overestimate the risks of other family members becoming affected, and this overestimation can influence level of concern about existing children and important life decisions, such as whether to have children. Specifically, those who overestimate risk for family members are more likely to make decisions about having fewer or no children, or to make significant changes to their parenting approach, home environment, and exposure to "harmful" environments in an effort to reduce risk. Clinicians who open a discussion with clients and families about causes of psychiatric illness and risk may facilitate the development of more accurate risk perceptions that could assist clients in making important life decisions.

- *OK, I'm convinced. But how do I know when to initiate discussions about cause of illness or family risk?*

Sometimes it will be easy to recognize when an individual might benefit from a discussion about the causes of psychiatric illness and risks for other family members to be affected. Readily recognizable questions and statements that you might hear from your clients or their family members include:

"Why did I develop a psychiatric illness?"

"Why is there psychiatric illness in my family?"

"I want children, but I'm concerned that they may develop the same psychiatric illness as me."

"Should I be concerned about my own/my children's mental health, now that I have a family member who is affected?"

In other circumstances it may be more difficult to recognize when individuals or families might benefit from a discussion about causes of illness and family risk. This might be particularly true for individuals and families who have already generated their own explanations that invoke internalized stigma, guilt, and shame. In such cases people may feel defensive when talking about the origins of illness because the cause to which they attribute the illness makes them feel guilty or scared to think about risks for family members. Clients who have strong beliefs about the cause being purely genetic may resist learning about the environmental components to illness for fear of feeling responsible for it. However, they may be more likely to overestimate the risks of family members being affected (e.g., feeling certain that their children will develop a psychiatric illness), and so may experience relief to know that it is not a foregone conclusion that their child will develop psychiatric illness.

Sometimes "throw-away" comments indicate that affected individuals and their family members are struggling to understand cause, or that they have attributed the cause to someone or something that is causing them or others distress. Examples of such statements might include:

"If only he hadn't done that [taken drugs, started hanging with the wrong crowd, broken up with girlfriend], he wouldn't be ill now."

"I don't want these medications—if I wasn't such a weak person, I could just try harder and I'd get better myself."

"If only I had known that this illness was in the family before I had my son!"

"I wish I had been there to prevent the accident, because then she would never have had that head injury and she wouldn't be like this now."

"I sometimes wonder if I hadn't divorced her father when she was small, would this still be happening to her?"

"I'm not interested in [stress management/CBT/psychoeducation]. Loads of people in my family have this illness, so obviously it's in my makeup—so I don't see how therapy can help."

Responding to statements such as these with an offer to discuss the causes of psychiatric illness could make a real difference to the individuals in question.

Essentially, you can prepare to begin the dialogue about causes of psychiatric illness and risks to other family members as soon as your client understands his or her diagnosis, even if he or she has not overtly requested the information. However, it is necessary to recognize the importance of timing such a discussion. There have been no empirical investigations into when (in relation to initial diagnosis) it is best to broach this topic with clients and families, but obviously, some commonsense judgments can be made. For example, the family who is in the throes of dealing with a teen's first active episode of psychosis and who is struggling to manage the associated day-to-day issues is probably not in the best position to engage in such a discussion. If your client is currently doing well but has not yet asked you about why the illness occurred, it may be because he or she is overwhelmed and has not considered how best to verbalize this need. Your client is likely to welcome a discussion with you about the causes of his or illness. In our experience, the optimal timing varies from family to family, but it is usually necessary for the client and family to accept the reality of a psychiatric illness before they benefit from discussing these issues.

PART I

TALKING WITH FAMILIES

The Basics

CHAPTER ONE

Genetics 101

In this chapter we provide a brief review of the evidence that genes are important contributing factors in the development of psychiatric illness. We define some of the basic terms that are commonly used in genetics. We then outline some of the basic principles and central concepts of genetics, and briefly review common research techniques. We describe how individual genetic factors seem to confer vulnerability to a broad range of psychiatric illnesses, and we list genetic syndromes that can be associated with increased risks for psychiatric illness. This information provides a foundation that will allow you to build an understanding of the more complex issues specific to psychiatric illness.

Genetics Terminology: The Basics

- *DNA:* Deoxyribonucleic acid is the medium in which the body's instructions regarding growth, development, and functioning are contained. DNA is a large molecule that is constructed from subunits, called *nucleotides*, that are arranged together in a chain. Each nucleotide is made up of three components, two of which are always the same. The third, variable component is called a *base*. There are four possible bases in DNA: adenine, guanine, thymine, and cytosine (often simply represented as A, G, T, and C). The instructions for growth, development, and functioning of all living organisms arise from the arrangement of nucleotides containing these four bases in different sequences and in chains of different lengths. Each chain of nucleotides has a partner chain, and each base in each nucleotide on one chain is bound to a base in a nucleotide on the partner chain. There is strict pairing of bases. A always binds to T, and C always binds with G. The two chains are tightly bound together in a twisting structure called a *double helix.*

- **Genome:** The word *genome* refers to the entire DNA sequence for an organism. Humans have a genome that is made up of approximately 3 billion base pairs. Most human cells (with a few exceptions) contain two copies of the genome, so each human cell contains about 6 billion base pairs of DNA. If we were to lay out all of the 6 billion base pairs of DNA in one human cell end-to-end, it would stretch for about 12 feet.

- **Chromosome:** To fit the 3 billion base pair human genome into a single human cell, the DNA molecules have to be very tightly packed. A chromosome is simply a tight package of DNA. The human genome is arranged into 23 pairs of chromosomes. Eggs and sperm (*gametes*) each have only one copy of each chromosome, such that when they combine together at conception, the new embryo is comprised of cells that contain the correct number of chromosomes (23 pairs). Thus, we all inherit one copy of each of our 23 pairs of chromosomes from our mothers, and the other copy of the pair from our fathers. Twenty-two of the pairs of human chromosomes are called *autosomes* and are identified by number (1–22). The 23rd pair contains the sex chromosomes, designated X and Y. In this last pair, females have two X chromosomes, and males have one X chromosome and one Y chromosome. Thus, females' eggs will always contain a single X chromosome, whereas males have sperm that contain an X chromosome and sperm that contain a Y chromosome.

- **Gene:** A gene is a section of DNA on a chromosome that typically contains instructions about how to make a protein, out of which our bodies are made. Humans are thought to have 20–25 thousand different genes. As each cell contains two copies of each chromosome, one from the mother and one from the father, there are also two copies of each gene. Though this is an oversimplification, in general, genes direct human growth and development and/or they allow the organism to respond to changes in the environment.

- *Genetic variation (or variant):* Variations in DNA sequences occur in many different forms. The smallest kind of genetic variation occurs when one DNA base is exchanged for another (this is known as a single nucleotide polymorphism, or SNP), but one or more DNA base(s) (and sometimes millions) can be deleted, duplicated, or moved (*translocated*). Variations can occur within the genes and in sections of DNA that do not contain genes. Genetic variations can be beneficial to the organism, benign (having no detrimental impact on the organism), or pathogenic. Some genetic variations are very rare and others are very common. Each human has many different genetic variations, including SNPs and larger variations that involve deletion, duplication, or translocation. Most of these do us no harm, but some of them may influence our risk for illness.

- *Alleles:* There are two copies of the human genome in each cell— one copy from each parent. Thus, there are two copies of DNA sequence for any given location in the genome; in some cases the maternally- and paternally-derived sequences at that particular location are identical, but in other cases the sequences vary. When the two copies exist in different forms, they are called alleles.

- *Genetic susceptibility:* The concept of genetic susceptibility is key to understanding the etiology of common disorders, including psychiatric disorders. Genetic susceptibility refers to the notion that genetic variations increase the risk of particular disorders, but are not sufficient to independently cause the disorder.

- *Complex (or multifactorial) traits and disorders:* Complex traits arise as a result of the combined effects of genetic and environmental contributions. Complex traits include things like intelligence and height, as well as traits associated with health and illness. Common illnesses such as asthma, diabetes, cancer, heart disease, and arthritis are usually complex disorders. These disorders are distinct from single-gene disorders in that genetic variations alone are usually insufficient to cause the illness, although they are usually necessary for the condition to develop. Unlike the traditional conceptualization of single-gene disorders, complex disorders usually arise as a result of the combined effects of several different genetic variations interacting with environmental factors.

The term *complex disorder* acknowledges that there are differences between individuals in terms of the specific factors contributing to the development of illness. For example, one individual with bipolar disorder may have risk genes *A*, *B*, and *C*, whereas another individual with the same condition may have risk genes *X*, *Y*, and *Z*. This phenomenon is known as *genetic heterogeneity*. When considering complex disorders, it is usually quite challenging to determine the chance that the child of an affected individual might have the same condition. Not only are the effects of the environment important, but also the simple statistics used to determine risks for single-gene disorders that are based on the segregation of alleles to subsequent generations do not work for complex disorders. This is because although each allele that confers susceptibility must segregate in families, the disorder does not track predictably with the susceptibility alleles because disorder onset requires multiple genes and environmental risk factors. Thus, the segregation of any single gene that confers susceptibility will not directly relate to the appearance of the illness in the family. Figure 1.1 diagrams familial agregation of psychiatric disorders.

- *Genetic syndrome:* A genetic syndrome is a group of features that occurs together with a known or assumed underlying genetic cause. There are a number of genetic syndromes that include psychiatric features as part of a constellation of features. These syndromes are caused by a specific change to one gene or chromosomal region.

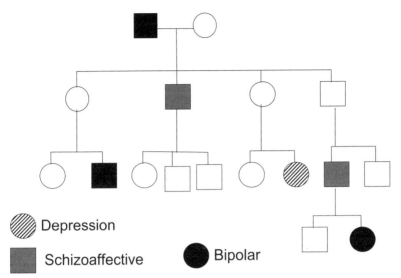

Figure 1.1. Pedigree showing multifactorial inheritance. In this family, a couple, one of whom has bipolar disorder (at top of picture), has four children. One of these children is affected with schizoaffective disorder, and all four of these children have children of their own. Although none of the children of the individual with schizoaffective disorder developed any psychiatric illness, one of his nephews has bipolar disorder, another has schizoaffective disorder, and one of his nieces has depression. In the fourth generation (three generations removed from the original individual with bipolar disorder), bipolar disorder emerges again in a child of an individual with schizoaffective disorder. In summary, this pedigree clearly shows aggregation (or clustering) of psychiatric illness in the family, but the pattern of inheritance is not clear—that is, the illnesses do not track predictably through the family, and multiple related disorders manifest.

Table 1.1 provides several examples of such genetic syndromes. Even taken together, these syndromes account for only a very small proportion of all psychiatric illnesses.

Strong scientific data support the idea that psychiatric illnesses are typically caused by the **combined influences of both genetic and environmental contributions**. The full range of, and exact

Table 1.1. Examples of Genetic Syndromes That May Present with Psychosis

Velocardiofacial (22q deletion) syndrome
Huntington disease
Prader–Willi syndrome
Wilson disease
Acute intermittent porphyria
Ornithine transcarbamylase (OTC) deficiency (female carriers)
Mitochondrial disorders
Tay Sachs (late onset)
Niemann–Pick, type C
X-linked adrenoleukodystrophy
Metachromatic leukodystrophy

Up to date information about all of these syndromes can be found at: www.ncbi
.nlm.nih.gov/sites/GeneTests/review

mechanisms by which, genetic factors contribute to psychiatric ill-nesses remain to be identified, as do many of the environmental factors. We are only beginning to appreciate the complexity of inter-actions between different combinations of genes and environmental factors (we discuss gene and environment interaction in Chapter 4). With so many open questions, some clients and family members might want to know more about the evidence that genetic factors contribute to the development of psychiatric illnesses. Because it can be very helpful for clinicians to feel confident in the information that they provide to their clients, and because some clients like to understand how we know what we do about the causes of these ill-nesses, we describe some of the studies from which we draw the conclusion that genes and environment are both important in the contributing to the development of psychiatric illnesses.

The first thoughts that psychiatric illnesses may be influenced by genes came about as a result of the observation that family members of individuals with psychiatric illness seemed to be more likely to develop similar mental health problems themselves. Three different types of research studies have shed light on the question of whether genes contribute to the development of psychiatric illness; we de-scribe each of these briefly below.

Family Studies

Family studies of psychiatric illness compare the rate of occurrence of a particular psychiatric illness in the first-degree relatives of an affected individual to the rate of occurrence of the same illness in a control population (e.g., a population of first-degree relatives of unaffected individuals). This kind of comparison generates data regarding the degree to which psychiatric illnesses aggregate (cluster more often than expected by chance) within families. Such studies have shown that, to a greater (e.g., schizophrenia) or lesser (e.g., major depression) degree, all psychiatric illnesses aggregate within families (Gottesman et al., 2010). Family studies have also shown that the first-degree relatives of affected individuals have risk for more than just the disorder diagnosed in the affected individual (Berrettini, 2000). Once a psychiatric disorder manifests in a family, close relatives are at increased risk for a range of other disorders that seem to share common risk factors (Lichtenstein et al., 2009).

While family studies can show that psychiatric illnesses cluster in families, they cannot be used to address the question of whether this clustering is attributable to familial genetic factors or to shared, familial environmental factors. Thus, although family studies provide circumstantial evidence that genetics is important in the development of psychiatric illness, they cannot be conclusive.

Twin Studies

Twin studies are helpful in attempting to disentangle the relative contributions of genetics and environment to a particular characteristic, such as psychiatric illness. Twin studies take advantage of the similarities and differences between identical and nonidentical twins. Identical twins share 100% of their genetic information because both embryos arise from the splitting of a single fertilized egg (zygote) early during development. In research, identical twins are referred to as monozygotic (MZ) twins. Nonidentical twins, on the other hand, share on average 50% of their genetic information (the same degree of genetic similarity that is found between non-twin siblings). The two embryos arise from two sperm simultaneously fertilizing two eggs. They are referred to as dizygotic (DZ) twins. Both MZ and DZ twins, of course, are born at the same time, to the same parents, and share an intrauterine environment. Twin studies are based on the assumption that the environments of MZ and DZ twins share the same degree of similarity.

Twin studies of mental illness compare "concordance rates" for specific psychiatric illnesses between MZ and DZ twins. A twin pair is considered to be concordant if both twins have the same psychiatric illness, and discordant if only one twin is affected. For characteristics that are entirely attributable to genetic variation, if one MZ twin is affected, the co-twin will always have the same characteristic, and if one DZ twin is affected, the co-twin will have a 50% (1 in 2) chance of having the same characteristic. If, on the other hand, a particular characteristic is entirely attributable to the effects of a shared environmental factor, MZ and DZ twins will have the same concordance rate. Thus, we can infer that genes play a role in the determination of any characteristic for which concordance rates in MZ twins are greater than those in DZ twins. Without exception, for the psychiatric illnesses that have been studied using this methodology, the concordance rates in MZ twins are greater than in DZ twins, but the MZ concordance rate is always less than 100% (Cardno et al., 1999; Smoller & Finn, 2003). From this, we can infer that genes contribute to the development of psychiatric illness. Further, the familial aggregation observed in family studies is probably attributable primarily to shared genetic factors, but the environment must also be important. Specifically, twin studies show that nonshared environmental risk factors (i.e., factors experienced differently by siblings) are more important in causing illness than are shared environmental risk factors (Tsuang, Stone, & Faraone, 2001).

Twin studies allow the derivation of *heritability estimates*, which are statistical expressions of the quantitative contribution of genetic variations to a characteristic. Some psychiatric illnesses, such as schizophrenia and bipolar disorder, have been shown to have some of the highest heritability estimates found in the complex disorders, and thus the genetic contribution to these conditions (at a population level) is thought to be substantial (Cardno et al., 1999). Heritability estimates for conditions such as panic disorder and major depression are considerably lower—closer to heritability estimates that we see in most other common medical disorders (Levinson, 2006). It is important to remember that because heritability estimates refer to the contribution of genes to a characteristic at the level of the population, we cannot then make inferences about the relative contributions of genes and environment in an individual. A useful analogy is that of childbearing. Specifically, in a given population, couples might have an average of 2.4 children. Of course, no couple will have precisely 2.4 children. In the same way, for a characteristic that has an estimated heritability of 70%, we cannot assume that the cause of this characteristic in a particular individual is 70% genetic and 30% environmental. A heritability of 70% means that 70% of the *differences* in the characteristics among a group of individuals are due to genetic differences among the group. In essence, we know that there is a large amount of interindividual variation in terms of the relative quantitative contributions of genes and environment to psychiatric illness.

Twin studies provided some of the most compelling early data about the relative importance of genes and environment in the onset of major psychiatric disorders. Twin studies are still being used in psychiatric research to evaluate more discrete, etiologically- or clinically-homogeneous groups for research, and to evaluate sex differences in the etiology of particular disorders (Cardno et al., 1999; Smoller & Finn, 2003).

Adoption Studies

Adoption studies investigate the rates of psychiatric illnesses in adopted children in relation to the rates found in their biological and adoptive parents. These kinds of studies can contribute substantially to the endeavor of disentangling the relative contributions of genes and environment to the development of a psychiatric illness. A limitation is that

they can obviously occur only in a naturalistic setting (i.e., the environment cannot be purposefully manipulated), which causes inherent
limitations. Even so, adoption studies have been employed to great effect in the investigation of contributions to schizophrenia and bipolar
disorder (as reviewed in Smoller & Finn, 2003). Adoption studies can
compare the rate of psychiatric disorders among a group of children
adopted away from affected mothers very shortly after birth to the rate
of the same illness among children adopted away from unaffected parents, or compare the rate of psychiatric illness in biological and adoptive parents of adopted individuals with psychiatric illness. As reviewed
by Ingraham and Kety (2000), the rate of schizophrenia in children
adopted away from affected mothers was approximately the same as
the rate one would expect had the children been raised with their biological parents, and adopted children with schizophrenia had a substantially higher rate of schizophrenia among their biological relatives
than adoptive relatives. These findings support the hypothesis that genetic factors contribute to the development of schizophrenia, and that
growing up with an affected parent does not cause the illness.

Summary of the Evidence Supporting the Involvement
of Genes in the Cause of Psychiatric Illness

Family, twin, and adoption studies show that psychiatric illnesses cluster in families and that this clustering is primarily due to the presence
of shared genetic vulnerability. Thus, these studies support the hypothesis that genetic variation is an important contributing factor to the
development of psychiatric illnesses. However, these studies also indicate that there is an important role for environmental risk factors, especially nonshared environmental risk factors. Further, although it is
clear that psychiatric illnesses cluster in families, this clustering is usually not of discrete, specific, single diagnoses. Instead, more typically,
one family may have members who have a range of diagnoses, such as
a family that includes a relative with schizophrenia, who brought the
family to attention, but also includes relatives with depression, anxiety, and alcoholism.

Though family, twin, and adoption studies provide a large amount of data about the importance of genes in psychiatric illness, they tell us nothing about the specific gene variations involved. In the next sections, we review concepts and terms that are used in genetics, and then we present a review of the approaches that have been used in attempts to identify the specific genes and genetic variations that can contribute to the development of psychiatric illness.

Efforts to Identify Genetic Variants That Contribute to Psychiatric Illnesses

Over the years, many different approaches have been used in the difficult pursuit of identifying the genes that contribute to the development of psychiatric illnesses. Researchers have identified several genetic variants that seem to be capable of increasing risk for psychiatric illness. Most of these risk-increasing variants seem to play a very small role in the overall risk for psychiatric illness. In addition, most of the variants identified to date are implicated as risk factors for more than one psychiatric outcome. For example, variants have been identified as increasing risk to both schizophrenia and bipolar disorder (Craddock et al., 2006; Post, 2007). This is not entirely unexpected, since there are shared features between psychiatric disorders, and diagnostic boundaries are not based on biological differences. Though progress in identifying genetic variants that increase risk is exciting, there is still a long way to go in terms of deriving clinically useful information from genetic test results.

Until recently, there were two primary approaches to the genetic study of psychiatric illnesses: linkage and association studies. More recently, new techniques and tools such as genome-wide association studies (GWAS), copy-number variation (CNV) analysis, and methylation analysis have provided new avenues for investigating psychiatric illnesses.

A comprehensive discussion of all of the laboratory methods that are used to aid in the study of genetic variation that may contribute to the development of psychiatric illness is beyond the scope of this book. However, we do provide descriptions of some of the most frequently used research approaches below. These descriptions can serve as foundational information that might increase your comfort level when reading the research literature and participating in related continuing education, as well as when discussing genetics and psychiatric illnesses with clients.

Linkage Studies

Linkage studies are based on the principle that the region of a chromosome that contains the gene responsible for causing a condition will be inherited together with the disease through multiple generations of a family (see Schork et al., 2007). Linkage studies can be used to identify particular regions of chromosomes that are more likely to contain genetic variations that increase the risk of, or indeed cause, a particular condition. This kind of research has been used to great effect to identify the genes that are responsible for causing single-gene disorders (e.g., Huntington's disease (Gusella et al., 1983), but because psychiatric illnesses are genetically heterogeneous and complex, linkage studies have proven less useful in identifying genes that are important in the development of psychiatric illnesses.

Association Studies

Association studies are based on the principle that a genetic variation that is important in the development of a psychiatric illness will appear more frequently in a population of individuals with that disorder than in a control population of individuals who are not affected (Cardon & Bell, 2001) . There are two primary ways in which genetic variations (or suspected genes, called *candidate genes*) have been selected for testing by way of traditional association study. The first involves selecting a genetic variation based on its chromosomal location within a previously identified area of linkage to the disorder of interest. This is

known as the *positional* candidate gene approach. The second involves selecting a genetic variation for association testing based on its
occurrence in a gene that encodes a protein whose function is theoretically important in the development of the disorder of interest (e.g.,
a genetic variation in a dopamine receptor might, theoretically, be important in the development of a psychiatric illness). This approach to
selecting candidate genes or variations to test is known as the *functional* candidate gene approach.

Genome-Wide Association Studies

Genome-wide association studies (GWAS) involve simultaneously per-
forming association studies (as described above) of hundreds of different genetic variations distributed across the entire genome (Corvin et
al., 2009). It is not necessary to have a hypothesis to test a specific
functional or positional candidate gene, because it is possible to test
genetic variations distributed across the entire genome at once. Any
genetic variation that occurs more frequently in a population of individuals with a given condition is said to be "associated" with that illness. In order to be able to run valid statistical comparisons between
groups of affected and unaffected individuals in GWAS studies, it is
necessary to have huge numbers of study participants (thousands in
the affected group, and thousands in the control group). The ability of
GWAS to identify genetic variants that increase risk for psychiatric disorders depends on the actual genetic architecture of specific psychiatric disorders (see Cichon et al., 2009).

Copy-Number Variation Analysis

Copy-number variation (CNV) analysis involves the evaluation of a special type of genetic variation. CNVs are sections of DNA (ranging in
size from 1,000 to 1 million DNA base pairs) that may be present in
different numbers (as a result of deletions or duplications) between
individuals (Merikangas et al., 2009). A CNV region may include a sin-

gle gene or many different genes. As with other types of genetic varia-tion, it appears that we all have CNVs. Often these do not have a negative impact on our health, but sometimes CNVs can influence our risk for a particular illness. The principles and strategies used when in-vestigating the potential role of CNVs in mental illness are much the same as those used in association studies: a CNV that is important in the development of a psychiatric illness will appear more frequently in a population of individuals with that disorder than in a control popula-tion of individuals who are not affected.

Methylation Analysis

Methylation of DNA is one of the mechanisms by which the amount of protein produced by a particular gene is regulated. When a gene is methylated, the amount of protein that it produces is reduced. Methy-lation studies can be used to investigate the extent to which specific genes are methylated in relation to risk for psychiatric illness (Iwamoto & Kato, 2009), using the principle that a methylation pattern that is important in the development of a psychiatric illness will appear more frequently in a population of individuals with that disorder than in a control population of individuals who are not affected. The extent to which some genes are methylated seems to be determined, at least in part, by specific environmental factors or experiences (Murgatroyd et al., 2009). To put it another way, methylation of DNA is potentially one of the mechanisms by which environmental exposures can in-crease vulnerability to psychiatric illness. We discuss this in more de-tail in Chapter 4.

Summary of Efforts to Identify and Locate Genetic Variants That Contribute to Psychiatric Illnesses

Psychiatric illnesses are complex (or multifactorial) disorders; defini-tive identification of specific genetic variations that can contribute to the development of a psychiatric illness has been confounded by what appears to be substantial heterogeneity. Two types of heterogeneity can potentially confound investigation of psychiatric illness: genetic and clinical heterogeneity. Using traditional genetic approaches of linkage and association, *genetic heterogeneity* (i.e., variation between affected individuals in the genetic factors that contribute to illness) makes it more difficult to definitively identify genetic variants that can increase risk. In addition, the more *clinical heterogeneity* there is in a population (i.e., clinical variation between individuals with the same diagnosis), the harder it is to identify genetic variants that increase risk for a particular characteristic. Thus far, the genetic variants that have been identified do not seem to confer vulnerability exclusively to one specific psychiatric diagnosis. Instead it seems that these variations increase vulnerability to psychiatric illness more generally, or to a particular type of psychiatric problem, such as psychosis or mood disturbance. In such circumstances, replication of study findings by independent groups becomes very important—and this replication has proven to be a challenge in psychiatric disorders.

The recent evolution of technology that makes GWAS possible, the discovery of CNVs and appreciation of their implications on health, our ability to evaluate methylation patterns, and the accumulation of very large collections of DNA samples from affected and unaffected individuals are already proving very promising in the effort to hone in on specific genetic variations that can confer an increased risk for psychiatric illness. It appears that some genetic variants that are important in the development of psychiatric illnesses are common in the population, but individually, each has only a small effect on overall risk for illness. Other genetic variants are very rare in the population but confer a large risk to those in whom they are present. It is likely that there are many genetic variants left to identify that can increase vulnerability to psychiatric illness, and our understanding of exactly *how* genetic variants confer risk is unclear. This is an area of rapid development. For the latest findings, you can look at websites such as *www.nimh*

.nih.gov and *www.schizophreniaforum.org*, which provide the most up-to-date information about the roles of specific genetic variations in illness pathogenesis.

At this point, there are no genetic tests available that have confirmed clinical validity and utility in predicting onset of psychiatric illness, diagnosing psychiatric illness, or determining best treatment for psychiatric illness (see Chapter 11 for full discussion). We anticipate that this will change, at least for a subset of families, in the near future.

What You Can Say to Clients and Family Members about Genetics and Psychiatric Illness

"Genes are the instructions that tell the body how to grow, develop, and function."

Starting with a brief general introduction to the topic of genetics helps people to better integrate the more complex concepts that may be presented later. Because people learn best when a variety of different educational modalities is used, it can be very helpful to include visual aids when describing that genes are special sequences of DNA that contain instructions that tell the body how it should grow, develop and function, and that gene products respond to changes in the environment.

"Genetic variations are changes in DNA, and variations in genes can cause changes in how the body grows, develops, functions, and responds to the environment."

Helping people to understand the relationship between genetic variations and the body as a whole can be helpful in establishing the foundations for your explanation about how genes and genetic variations affect the brain. It is important to point out that we all have lots of genetic variations, that they can happen randomly, and that having them is normal. Usually these genetic variations do not have a noticeable impact on how our bodies grow, develop, and function, but occasionally, a genetic variation does cause an increased or reduced chance of developing a particular illness or group of illnesses.

> *"Some genes instruct the body in how to make chemicals that are important in the brain. If genetic variations occur in these genes, the result may be too much or too little of important brain chemicals, or brain chemicals that don't work adequately—any of which can cause a chemical imbalance in the brain."*

One of the explanations for the origins of psychiatric illness with which people tend to be quite familiar is that these illnesses are caused by a chemical imbalance in the brain. Relating your explanation of the cause of psychiatric illness to the existing ideas people may have helps to engage people in discussion and to accept and retain new knowledge.

> *"Genetic variations do not usually cause psychiatric illness, but they can make a person more vulnerable to one. The genes that can make a person more vulnerable to psychiatric illness may be referred to as 'risk genes.'"*

This is a key concept. Some clients might prefer the term *risk* or *vulnerability*, whereas others prefer *susceptibility* or *predisposition* to psychiatric illness. Still others respond best to the idea of having a genetically-based sensitivity to their environment that makes them more likely to develop psychiatric illness.

> *"What is inherited is a vulnerability to psychiatric illness, rather than psychiatric illness itself."*

This is another key concept that directly relates to the previous point. Although the distinction here is subtle, it is very important. Psychiatric illnesses arise as a result of the combined effects of several different genetic variations *acting together with, and in response to,* the environment, so no one factor itself causes the illness. It can sometimes be helpful to compare the differences between vulnerability arising from risk genes to autosomal dominant or recessive disorders that are caused by a single genetic variation.

> *"The greater the genetic risk, the more vulnerable a person is to developing psychiatric illness. It is likely that everyone has some vulnerability to psychiatric illness."*

Some people have a large amount of genetic risk for mental illness, and others have a small amount of genetic risk; most people have a moderate vulnerability to psychiatric illness.

Issues That Clients and Family Members Might Raise about Genetics and Psychiatric Illness

"How do you know that genes are important in the development of psychiatric illness?"

We know that psychiatric illnesses tend to cluster in families; this means that relatives of someone with a psychiatric illness are more likely than relatives of someone who is unaffected to develop a psychiatric illness. On its own, this is not enough to tell us that genes are important in psychiatric illness, because it could be that family members share an environment that makes them more likely to develop psychiatric illness. But studying twins can help us work out whether genes are important in the development of an illness. There are two kinds of twins: identical and nonidentical (you may have heard the term *fraternal* used when referring to nonidentical twins). Identical twins share 100% of their genes, and nonidentical twins share 50% of their genes. We can use this difference between identical and nonidentical twins to see if genes are important in causing an illness. If genes play an important role in the emergence of a particular illness, we would expect that if one twin has illness, the other twin would be affected more often if they were identical than if they were fraternal. This is exactly what we see for psychiatric illnesses, which tells us that genes are important.

"How do genetic variations happen?"

Genetic variations happen naturally, for many different reasons, and each of us has many different types of variation in our genes. Because genes are passed through the family, from parent to child, genetic variations can be passed on in the same way.

"Everyone says I look the same as my sibling who has a psychiatric illness. Am I more likely to develop a psychiatric illness than our other sibling, who looks nothing like him?"

No. The genes that control our appearance are unlikely to be the same ones that contribute to risk for psychiatric illness. We each have 20–25,000 genes, and just because you share some similarities in genes that contribute to appearance, it does not mean that you will share the same risk genes for psychiatric illness.

"Can I have genetic testing to tell me whether I will develop psychiatric illness?"

Studies have found evidence for considerable interest among affected individuals and their family members in the prospect of genetic testing for psychiatric illness (Coors, 2005; Meiser et al., 2008; Trippitelli et al., 1998). Any genetic testing that may become available for psychiatric illnesses will only be able to provide information about the probability of a person developing a disorder, rather than a definitive categorical answer. Interest in genetic testing has been found to be greater when categorical answers (e.g., yes, no) are provided than when only probabilistic answers (i.e., "You have a 30% chance") are given (Meiser et al., 2008). Experience with other disorders (including Huntington's disease and hereditary breast and ovarian cancer syndromes) suggests that the interest in genetic testing for a condition is usually greater when its availability remains hypothetical than when the test actually becomes clinically available (Evers-Kiebooms & Decruyenaere, 1998). Nevertheless, the important message for people who ask this question is that genetic testing for psychiatric illness is unlikely to ever predict exactly who will and who will not develop psychiatric illness, because the environment contributes to risk, too. At the moment we do not know all of the different risk genes for psychiatric illness, and we also do not yet understand how the different risk genes might interact with each other. At this point, genetic testing is not very helpful in predicting who will and will not develop mental illness.

> *"Is it the risk genes for psychiatric illness that make me/my affected family member so creative?"*

It is certainly possible that the genes that make a person more vulnerable to developing psychiatric illness have more positive effects too— like making people more creative. At this point, we cannot definitively answer this question.

> *"No one else in my family has this illness, so are genes not important in the psychiatric illness in my family?"*

Most people with psychiatric illnesses such as schizophrenia or bipolar disorder have no affected family members. This does not mean that genes are not important in the development of these illnesses in these families. In fact, this is what we would expect to see, given that risk genes do not *cause* psychiatric illness. Remember, just because a person has a large number of risk genes does not mean that he or she will develop a psychiatric illness; without the contributing environmental factors, he or she may remain healthy. So, although other family members may be unaffected, they may still have a large number of risk genes. Alternatively, it is possible that both of the parents of the individual who developed the psychiatric illness have an average amount of risk genes, and that neither of them ever developed the illness themselves, but that their child (who went on to develop psychiatric illness) inherited all of the risk genes from both parents, and so was much more vulnerable to developing psychiatric illness than was either parent.

"Is there any way I could prevent passing on risk genes to my child?"

It can be very important for people to understand that we have no control over the genes that we pass on to our children. Most parents would like to be able to pass on what they consider to be their "good" characteristics to their children, without passing on the characteristics that they consider to be less desirable. Whether risk genes are passed on comes down to chance. This lack of control can be difficult for some people to accept, but can be a great relief in other circumstances—for example, when talking with parents of a child who has developed psychiatric illness.

"Can I do anything to change how many risk genes I have?"

There is no way to reduce the number of risk genes that we have for psychiatric illness. But, it is important to remember that genetic vulnerability alone does not usually cause psychiatric illness. Although we cannot change our genetic vulnerability, there may be things that we can do to reduce our risk for psychiatric illness. This topic is discussed in more detail in Chapters 4 and 8.

"I heard that schizophrenia and bipolar disorder are about 80% genetic. Is that true?"

One of the most widely misinterpreted concepts related to genetics and mental illness is heritability. *Heritability* is a statistical measure of the degree to which a particular condition is attributable to genetics— at the level of the population. It is true that schizophrenia and bipolar disorder have both been estimated to have heritabilities in the region of 80%, but it is important to remember that this is a population-based concept. For example, although *on average* (at a population level) couples may have 2.4 children, no individual couple will actually have 2.4 children. In much the same way, although these conditions have population-based heritabilities of about 80%, it is not correct to then assume that an individual with schizophrenia or bipolar disorder has that condition as a result of an 80% contribution of genes and a 20% contribution of the environment. At the level of individuals there is likely to be a huge range in the relative contribution of genetics to the development of the disorder.

Our Experience

One of the explanations for the causes of psychiatric illness that is the most familiar to affected individuals and their family members is that of "chemical imbalance in the brain." We have found that, while this explanation goes some way to helping people understand their illness, it is not a sufficiently deep or detailed explanation for many—particularly for those who are most interested in protecting themselves against future episodes of active illness, or protecting other family members who may be at higher risk. We are often confronted with questions such as "How did the chemicals in my brain become imbalanced?" Explaining that genetic variations can lead to different amounts of proteins, or to slight variations in the structure of proteins made by the body, and that these proteins might be neurotransmitter receptors and transporters, can help people make the connection between genetic variation and brain chemical imbalance. In our experience, this can be a real "aha moment."

Case Example

Deborah first experienced mental health problems in her mid-20s and shortly thereafter was diagnosed with schizoaffective disorder. Now 40, her mental health since that time has been generally poor. She felt that she should not need medications to be mentally healthy and was reluctant to take those prescribed by her psychiatrist. At the time I (JA) saw Deborah, she was an inpatient in a psychiatric ward as a result of a recent suicide attempt. Deborah wanted genetic counseling to better understand the causes of her mental illness. In recounting her story, Deborah identified a number of significant life stressors around the time she first experienced mental health problems, but told me that she attributed her illness to weak character, and that if she could only try harder, she would be OK; thus, her ongoing difficulties made her feel like a failure.

She gave me excellent information with which to construct a detailed psychiatric family history, which showed that both of her parents had experienced significant mental health problems themselves. I reviewed Deborah's own psychiatric family history with her and showed her that it was very likely that she had inherited genetic vulnerability to mental illness from both of her parents. She broke down into tears. Deborah had always assumed that her illness was a result of her own weak character. For Deborah, the evidence laid in front of her that genetics must have contributed something to the development of her illness lifted a debilitating and long-borne burden of self-blame. Later, Deborah told me that she also felt differently toward the notion of pharmacological treatment for her illness after learning about the causes of it. In her mind, if the cause was weak character, she felt it was entirely her responsibility to get better on her own, without medication. But if the cause was in part genetic, then a biological treatment made more sense to her.

CHAPTER TWO

Getting Started: Contracting

The process of providing counseling about the causes of psychiatric illness and risks for family members to become affected should begin with contracting and learning about your client's perceptions and objectives. In addition to establishing session boundaries (e.g., time), contracting makes explicit both your goals for the session and those of your client. The contracting process should include an investigation of your client's perceptions of his or her illness and of risks of family members becoming affected. This chapter includes information about identifying your own goals for counseling in this context and those of your client; the importance of exploring your client or family member's existing perceptions of cause, burden, illness control, and amount of family risk; and the importance of acknowledging our inability to provide certain information about personal cause and risk for family members to become affected.

Elucidating Your Client's Goals and Sharing Your Own

Contracting promotes your clients' autonomy by increasing their control over the process and the information discussed. The needs of your clients will differ based on their personal and family histories, their age and phase in life, and the reason(s) for concern. Some of your clients will primarily seek education, some will primarily seek psychological counseling around risk in the family, some will be most interested in discussions of early symptom identification and early intervention, and some will request risk assessment. Contracting allows individualization of timing and focus of the counseling process. Examples of how client goals for a session might be expressed follow:

> *Client*: "I would really like to understand why I got this illness when no one else in my family did."

> *Pregnant client*: "I would like to know more about the chance that this baby could get the same condition that I have, anything I can do during the pregnancy to reduce those chances, and whether I should stay on my medication during the pregnancy."

> *Client planning pregnancy*: "How much risk is there for me to have a baby with the same condition? I'm not sure if it is worth the risk or not. Is there any way to tell for sure? How will I stand the uncertainty, if I choose to have a baby?"

> *Client with at-risk children*: "I would like to know if I am right to be worried about my son. The pediatrician says he's doing fine, but I can't help but worry about what may happen, especially now that he's a teenager. How will I tell what's normal teenage behavior and what might be mood symptoms? What should I do if I get really worried?"

> *At-risk individual* (e.g., sibling of client): "I know I have an increased chance. But here's what worries me most: My sister never can tell when she's becoming symptomatic. I have to help her understand that she needs to get help. If I start having symptoms, who will help me? I can't stand the constant fear and checking into my own mind."

> *Potential adoptive parent when child has an affected biological parent*: "I was so excited to find out that they chose us to adopt the baby. But then we found out that the baby's mother has

schizophrenia. We just don't know what to do. We want a baby so badly, but schizophrenia is an awful disease. Is it worth the risk?"

All of these types of statements and questions provide an excellent opportunity to learn about your client's perceptions of his or her illness. Understanding your client's illness perceptions allows you to provide more targeted and effective counseling.

After you have determined the client's primary goals for the interaction, the contracting process also gives you a forum in which to explain other reasonable expectations for the encounter, or to share what you think might be most important or relevant for each client. You could present a topic that the client has not thought of; for example, you might say that you could discuss the importance of early symptom identification in at-risk children, and the client may be pleased to have the opportunity to learn this new and unexpected information. Or the client's goal might be to learn more about the risk of psychiatric illness in her child and how to maintain a low-stress home environment, while you might have a goal of helping the client develop a plan for child-care if she becomes symptomatic.

Assessing Perceptions of Illness and Family Risk

Illness perceptions play an important role in shaping an individual's response to information about the cause of a psychiatric illness and the risk of family members becoming affected. Identifying and understanding your client's illness perceptions allows you to provide more targeted and effective counseling. In addition, there is evidence that attempting to provide new information about the causes of psychiatric illness without first exploring existing perceptions is likely to be a relatively unsuccessful strategy (Skirton & Eiser, 2003). Illness perceptions may also play a role in treatment adherence. Some of the themes that have been shown to play a role in appraisals of illness risk include the following:

- *Burden*: Clients who perceive more burden as a result of the illness typically not only perceive risk to be higher but also tend to have less tolerance for risk.
- *Control*: Clients who perceive themselves as having less control over the onset of the illness in themselves/their children, and/or their illness symptoms and course, typically not only perceive risk to be higher but also tend to have less tolerance for risk.
- *Preconceptions about cause*: Clients' preconceptions about the cause of their illness/the illness in their family will affect how they receive information about the combination of genetic and environmental risk.
- *Preconceptions about risk for family members*: Clients' preconceptions of family risk before the genetic counseling session affect the way in which they receive information about genetic risk that is provided during the risk counseling.

Thus, it is important to discuss with your clients their perceptions and preconceptions of their own illness, including degree of burden and locus of control; their perceptions and preconceptions of the degree of illness burden and the locus of control experienced by others (including affected relatives as well as at-risk relatives); how likely they think it is that it will happen again in the family, and the rationale for their concern or lack of concern about family risk. Gathering this background information will help you to tailor your messages to each individual client and to anticipate areas of concern and reactions to information about causes of illness and risk.

Tips for Getting Started

It is our experience that regardless of the specific diagnosis, individuals with psychiatric illnesses and/or their family members and partners perceive their illnesses to involve some significant degree of burden, and it is common for clients to express fears about their ability to control symptoms or maintain their desired life course in the future.

A large proportion of individuals with psychiatric illness and their family members seem to intuitively appreciate that both genetics and life experiences are somehow involved in the emergence of psychiatric illnesses. Often, however, these pieces are seen as quite disparate, and it is difficult for clients to generate a coherent picture of how the illness arises. In addition, because at times the significance attached to the role of genetics or environment is dramatically overestimated, an exploration of these perceptions at the outset of the discussion allows for such potentially harmful misconceptions to be clarified and for correct perceptions to be reinforced and incorporated into a coherent whole later on in the session.

With regard to risk perception, in our practice we find that clients seeking genetic counseling perceive a general family vulnerability to psychiatric illness and appreciate that there is an increased risk in the family. Most of our clients are highly motivated to modify this vulnerability and reduce risks for relatives. However, our clients are self-selected and are likely to be those who appreciate the genetic contribution to psychiatric illness, in that they sought out a consultation with a genetics professional. We also are more likely to see families that include more than one affected individual. In general, when there are multiple affected family members, they rightly perceive an increased risk for relatives. It is not clear whether this perception is shared by the majority of clients encountered by mental health professionals. Research in less selected populations, however, backs up our experience that most clients and their relatives appreciate that risk is increased, and in fact often overestimate the risk (Austin et al., 2006; Quaid et al., 2001; Trippitelli et al., 1998).

As a clinician, you will be familiar with the transient and changeable nature of illness perceptions. This is also true for risk perceptions. Not only are perceptions likely to change over time, but clients may hold more than one incongruent belief about any aspect of their illness. Their perception of the salience of the information and their control over outcomes may affect their coping over time. For example, we have found that clients who are highly motivated to have children report that they "ignored" or "didn't think about" the risk to their children until after their childbearing was complete. Later, they may be quite concerned about the risk to existing children.

The coping efforts that clients use to deal with their own illness and their family risk also may have a significant effect on how interested they will be in discussions of cause and family risk, and how they will perceive information provided by health-care clinicians. In our research and clinical experience, we have found that some clients cope with risk to relatives by watching, preparing, and seeking information, while others cope by denial—by identifying reasons why their relatives are not at such significant risk (Peay et al., 2009). Your clients may, of course, use more than one coping strategy at a time, even when those strategies may seem to be conflicting, and they are likely to use different coping efforts over time.

What You Can Say to Clients and Family Members To Get Started

"We have an hour [insert correct time span] today to spend talking about some of the issues you are interested in—for example, what causes psychiatric illness, and how much risk there might be for other family members to be affected."

As with many other clinical interventions, identifying up-front how much time you can spend with your client discussing these issues on this particular occasion defines the boundaries of the session and is an important part of the contracting process. Let the client know if the discussion can continue at a later date.

"You told me that you were interested in learning more about what caused your illness. Do you have specific questions that

you would like to make sure we cover?" Or *"What motivated you*
to ask me about the causes of your illness?"

This beginning can open a dialogue about your client's goals for the
session, which are important to establish at the outset.

"What do you feel was responsible for causing your/your family
member's psychiatric illness?"

In addition to providing insight into an individual's existing level of
knowledge and allowing you to tailor the level of your discussion to
him or her, discussing the factors that the client or family member perceives to be contributing to the illness can identify accuracies that you
would seek to reinforce and affirm, as well as misconceptions that may
need correction. Indeed, if the individual's existing ideas about the
cause for psychiatric illness are not addressed in the context of the
new explanation that you provide, it is more difficult and less appealing for your client to integrate the new knowledge. If the client responds to this question with "I don't know," consider reframing the
question:

"Tell me about what was going on for you/your family member
just around the time you/they first got sick." Or *"Has anyone else*
in the family ever experienced similar problems?"

These additional questions can be really helpful in providing an opening for people to tell you about factors that they think are significant.

"Sometimes, people don't want to learn about the causes of
psychiatric illnesses because they are afraid that they will hear
that it is somehow their fault."

Many clients and family members think that there was something they
did or did not do that actually caused the illness. If you suspect this is

the case, opening a dialogue with a statement to this effect can be very helpful. For people who have heard or wondered about the role of family dynamics, personal weakness, or character flaws in causing psychiatric illness, it can be helpful to mention that there has been a lot of damaging misinformation over the years, and that you will help them sort out the likely causes from the unlikely ones.

"Sometimes people don't want to take psychiatric medications because they think that their illness is caused by fate or a weak character and so medications won't help."

When affected individuals or their family members do not ask about the causes of psychiatric illness, it may be because they have already established their own explanation. Sometimes this attribution for the cause of illness has observable manifestations or consequences. For affected individuals whose attributions lead them to feel "doomed," whether because the illness was "fated" to occur or so strongly genetic that there was no escape, treatment may seem futile and the individuals may not take their prescribed medication. In situations like this, where the behavioral consequence of an illness attribution is exposed, there is the potential for significant shifts in attitudes following the education gained in the session.

"Before we started talking about the causes of psychiatric illness, you told me that you were interested in talking about the risks that family members will be affected. Now that we have talked about causes, I thought I would check in and see if you are still interested in hearing about risks."

Checking in like this can be an excellent way to see how the preceding discussion about the causes of psychiatric illness was received, in addition to ensuring that you are positioning yourself to meet your client's needs regarding risk assessment. Importantly, this kind of checking in also preserves your client's right *not* to know. It may be the case that simply hearing that psychiatric illnesses are not entirely attributable to genes is sufficient for an individual to realize that there is a chance that his or her child/other relative would not be affected—which may be sufficient information for that client's needs.

> *"Although I will be giving you information about the chances for your children to be affected, should you decide to have any, I won't tell you what to do—for example, I won't make any statements about whether or not you should have children. I want to give you the best information that I can to help you make decisions that are right for you."*

It can be very helpful to state at the outset of the discussion that you aim to promote decision-making and autonomy and will not instruct your client about which choice to make on such important topics. Depending on your clinical role, clients might expect you to be directive, especially about decision-making or life planning. It can be useful to establish a common understanding about such issues at the beginning of a session.

> *"I was wondering if you might also be interested in learning about how to notice illness symptoms in at-risk relatives?"*

Once the client has expressed his or her goals for the session, you may feel that there are other topics that might also be useful to discuss. It may be that the client was unable to articulate the desire for information in this area, or alternatively, perhaps he or she was unaware that it was available as an option for discussion, so providing other suggestions may be helpful.

> *"It can be really hard to worry about the chances for yourself [other members of the family/your children] to develop a psychiatric illness."*

Adolescent and adult children and siblings of affected individuals often silently harbor worries that they may develop the same illness as their family member. Parents of young people who have been diagnosed with a psychiatric illness are often worried about the risks to their other children. Affected grandparents and grandparents with an affected child are often concerned about the risk to their grandchildren. And finally, diagnosed individuals who have young children are often deeply worried that their children will develop the same illness sometime in the future. These fears are frequently left unarticulated—in fact, in our experience, when such fears are articulated, many clients find that their health-care clinicians are unwilling to address them—and opening a conversation in this way combats the sense of isolation that people with these worries often face.

"Do you have a sense of the chance that [your child/other relative] will develop [psychiatric illness X]?"

We described above how important it is to assess a client's existing attributions of his or her illness prior to your providing new information about the causes of psychiatric illness. In the same way, it is important to inquire about your client's existing perception of risk prior to providing a risk assessment.

"It can be really helpful to base discussions about the cause of psychiatric illness or risks to family members on a detailed psychiatric family history. I can use this history to see if what we know about causes of psychiatric illness in general relates to you and your family. Would it be OK if we start by drawing out your family history?"

In the interest of helping the client understand the content of the session, it can be helpful to obtain permission to ask about potentially sensitive family history when these discussions are initiated, and briefly explain the purpose of the family history. Having an established therapeutic relationship with the client may facilitate your ability to obtain a more complete family history while maintaining a high level of client comfort.

Issues That Clients and Their Families May Raise

"What information can you offer me? What are the limitations of knowledge about the cause of my condition?"

Most clients understand that we do not have all of the answers about causes of and risks for psychiatric illness. These types of questions allow you to acknowledge the limitations of our understanding about the specific factors that contribute to psychiatric illness. It also provides an opportunity to educate more interested clients about why the answers have been so difficult for researchers to achieve. This discussion lays the groundwork for how clients may use the information provided during etiology and risk counseling.

"Am I right to be this worried? Can you reassure me?"

Clients may explicitly or implicitly communicate that they hope to be told that the risk to relatives is less than they anticipated. At the same time, many clients (especially parents) say that they would appreciate having their concerns confirmed; this can be an empowering experience for parents who know that there is risk in their family, but who have never had their knowledge and experience validated by a professional.

"Can you tell me why I have this illness? Can you tell me exactly what the chance is that this will happen again in my family?"

Clients may wish for definitive, clear-cut answers about causes of illness and degree of risk to family members. They may be disappointed to hear that, while we can provide up-to-date information about the causes of psychiatric illnesses in general terms, it currently is not possible to conclusively identify each one of the specific factors that contributes to the development of illness for any one individual. Our experience, however, is that clients are understanding about the scientific limitations and appreciate being given up-to-date, client-friendly information.

"I don't want to hear about risk to children because I already know that they would certainly have this same illness as me, so I'm not having any."

This kind of statement presents a difficult but not uncommon situation. The client obviously has a right not to know and, indeed, is telling you that he or she wishes not to know—but his or her decision is based on an assumption that is incorrect. In this situation, exploring with the client the basis for this assumption may be helpful. This kind of statement may be based on an assumption that the illness is entirely genetic in its origins. Simply asking whether the client has an interest in discussing the causes of this illness can allow conclusions to be revised based on this new information.

Our Experience

Case Example

Shelley remembered first hearing voices when she was 10 years old, but did not know that this was an unusual experience until years later. Shelley was diagnosed with schizophrenia in her teens. Now in her 30s, she came with her husband to see me (JA) for genetic counseling. She told me that she wanted to understand the cause of her illness because she could never comprehend why it was that she got sick and her sister didn't, despite the fact that they had had the same experiences. When I asked if there were specific questions she would like to have addressed, Shelley told me about her sister, who was 2 years younger. As children, they moved home multiple times, each time changing schools, and then when Shelley was 9, their parents divorced. Shelley found these experiences to be hugely stressful and emotionally difficult, and she attributed her illness entirely to them. However, her sister had had the same experiences and had not developed schizophrenia, so Shelley was confused and wanted me to explain why this might be. I offered to try to do this, and then asked if Shelley and her husband were considering a family, and whether she would also be interested in hearing about chances that her children would be affected. Despite her belief that her illness was the result of her difficult childhood experiences, Shelley had decided not to have children because she felt that they would be certain to develop schizophrenia. She also felt that her illness had a profoundly negative personal impact and was very burdensome to the entire family. She didn't want to bring someone else into the world who was "bound to suffer and make others suffer." Her husband, on the other hand, was interested in hearing about risks and asked Shelley if she would mind if I did tell them more about it. Shelley's attitude was that it couldn't be worse news than what she already thought, so she shrugged and agreed to talk about that too, to accomodate her husband's wishes. Shelley was initially reluctant to discuss family history. She couldn't imagine what use it would be because, she told me, no one else in the family had schizophrenia. She and her husband agreed that I could draw out their psychiatric family histories after I explained that it would help me to talk about known etiology of schizophrenia and about risks for family members to become affected. Shelley became increasingly interested in the discussion. Based on the process outlined in this chapter, we established a mutually agreed upon agenda for the session, and I developed a good idea about Shelley's perceptions of her illness. I felt that her sense of control over her illness was uncertain, but that she had more definite perceptions of burden and risk for family members to be affected. She gave me insight into her understanding of what had caused her illness, and I was able to refer to her understandings as I offered my explanations about etiology.

Case Example

Therese and Jon came to my (HP) service to learn about their family risk and the chance that their son and daughter might have obsessive–compulsive disorder (OCD) and depression. Jon had a personal history of OCD, and Therese had a strong family history of depression. They clearly articulated their desire to learn about the causes of depression and OCD, whether their children were at risk for one or both of the disorders, and what the quantitative magnitude of that risk would be. They brought up the idea of genetic testing, having recently seen a news report that described a research study on the genetics of OCD. They stated that the article said that "the gene for OCD" had been identified by researchers at a major university, and they wondered if genetic testing was available. I assured them that I would be able to provide a good deal of information about the disorders and the risk to their children based on their personal and family histories. I then informed them that genetic testing is not yet commercially or clinically available for OCD. I used the news report as a teaching tool to help them understand the complexity of the disorder and why identifying a risk gene (even assuming that the risk gene is truly involved in the disorder onset) may not provide clinically useful information in any one individual. The couple stated that they wished that such testing was available, but that they were very pleased to be able to get "as much information as you know" about why the disorders occur and how likely they were to develop in their children.

CHAPTER THREE

Taking a Family History

The psychiatric family history is the cornerstone of activities related to education and counseling about causes of psychiatric illness and risk for family members to be affected. In this chapter we provide tools and strategies for collecting a useful psychiatric family history. We begin by outlining the benefits of gathering a targeted psychiatric family history and describing some different options for formats that can be used to document the family history. In addition, we briefly review the accuracy of the self-reported family history and barriers to obtaining a psychiatric family history.

Goal and Benefits of Gathering a Psychiatric Family History

The goal of the psychiatric family history is to acquire accurate information about psychiatric symptoms and diagnoses, social history, and family function for all family members within at least three generations. The more complete the family history—the more complete the data about genetic, family, and environmental risk factors—the more comprehensively you can understand the causes of illness and risk in the family. The family history can allow you to personalize messages about causes of the illness, as is detailed in Chapter 4, and risk information, as is detailed in Chapters 5 and 6.

In addition to providing insight into the illness cause and magnitude of risk for relatives, the psychiatric family history offers information about family function and dynamics and may suggest the need for additional psychological support. Taking a family history is best considered as a process that is woven through the counseling session rather than as a discrete task that has a defined start and end within the session. During the process of gathering a family history, clients are likely to disclose personal and sometimes difficult information. Clients may have to revisit what they perceive to be poor life choices or difficult experiences with affected relatives, or reflect upon how their illness has affected family members. Especially when clients have children, guilt related to passing on (or potentially passing on) the disorder to the child can be significant. Thus, gathering a psychiatric family history might elicit feelings of sadness, guilt, anxiety, or anger in the client, and it is vital that you are prepared to respond supportively.

The information you collect during the family history may have implications for your client's diagnosis and treatment. It may provide clues about illness course; for example, symptoms of magical thinking and paranoia in a child of an individual with schizophrenia might be considered more worrisome than the same symptoms in the child of someone with no affected family members. You may also uncover information about comorbid disorders in the family, which may be of concern to your client. The history also provides clues about the most effective treatment modalities—what works for one relative is likely to work for another, since drug response is partially genetically mediated (see Chapter 12). In the most well known example, a family history of bipolar disorder should increase caution in using antidepressants in a depressed client, because he or she might be more vulnerable to conversion to mania after use (Joseph et al., 2009).

Especially if you have not yet established a therapeutic relationship with your client, the collection of a psychiatric family history can provide a way to build rapport. Beginning the session with the family history sets the stage for an interaction in which the client is heard throughout the counseling session; it is an interactive exercise that requires input from both the clinician and the client in a client-centered process. Family information gathering may be empowering for the client, allowing him or her to be the expert on family history. Your role in the family history documentation process is to act as a guide for your client, encouraging appropriate history and asking good follow-up questions.

Finally, the family history is an excellent teaching tool. We provide more information about how you can use the family history to teach clients about the causes of psychiatric illness and about risk to family members in Chapters 4 and 6.

Formats for Documenting a Family History

There are many different methods from which you can choose to obtain family history information. You could consider asking that clients provide family history information using a standardized checklist or survey, using a web-based family history tool, during an over-the-phone previsit interview, or you may obtain the information yourself during an office visit. Questionnaires, web-based family history tools, and over-the-phone interviews have the advantage of time efficiency and advance case preparation. It is good practice, however, to gather or at least review family history data in the presence of the client. Face-to-face collection allows you to make observations and gain more information about specific relatives of interest, perceptions of the disorder, family dynamics, and psychosocial factors. In practice, many clinicians use a combination of strategies, including asking clients to complete a checklist with basic information and then asking for more detailed information in the office, prompted by the answers the client provides on the checklist.

Regardless of how the family history is gathered, it is important to use a standardized format for documenting it. Family history data should have the following characteristics:

• Easy for other clinicians to interpret
• Easy to update
• Be dated and signed
• Make relationships between relatives clear
• Include information about both affected and unaffected relatives
• Include a key for any symbols or abbreviations.

Because family history changes over time, it is vital that you occasionally update the information.

In genetics settings, a standardized pedigree format is used to document family history information. The pedigree is a detailed pictorial representation of all the individuals in the family and their relationships. Typically, in genetics, males are represented as squares and females as circles (Bennett et al., 2008). Individuals within the same generation (e.g., brothers and sisters) are grouped together horizontally (e.g., at a constant measure on an imaginary y-axis) and different generations (e.g., parents and grandparents) are arranged vertically (e.g., each separate generation occupying a different constant measure on an imaginary y-axis), as shown in Figure 3.1. Benefits of using a standardized pedigree format include the following:

• The pedigree is familiar to most health clinicians.
• The biological relationships between individuals are clear.
• The pedigree includes affected and unaffected relatives.
• The pedigree makes patterns in the family more apparent (or shows the lack thereof).
• There are published recommendations for format and structure.
• It is an excellent teaching tool (as discussed in Chapters 4 and 6).

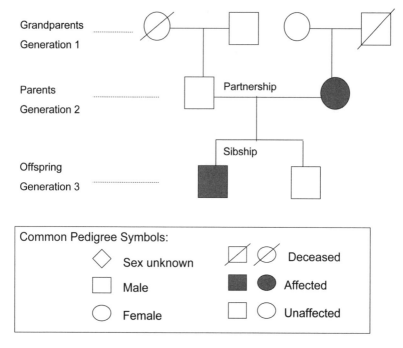

Grandparents
Generation 1

Parents
Generation 2   Partnership

Offspring
Generation 3

Sibship

Common Pedigree Symbols:

◇ Sex unknown   ⊠ ⊘ Deceased

□ Male   ■ ● Affected

○ Female   □ ○ Unaffected

Figure 3.1. Pedigree showing standardized symbols and layout. Note that each generation occupies a distinct horizontal line.

Alternative Methods for Documenting Psychiatric Family History

Family History Documentation Method 1: Narrative

In this example the information is conveyed in the format of a clinical report, as follows.

Brenda, age 32, attended counseling to discuss the causes of her mental health problems and the risks of future children having mental illness. Brenda has a history of severe depression, which began when she was about 16; she currently takes Paxil. Her mother (age 52) was diagnosed with depression at about 26 years of age, but she had been experiencing symptoms for several years prior to receiving a diagnosis. Mother also is currently treated with Paxil. Brenda's father has no mental illness history. Brenda's aunt (age 58) has a history of depression, She was diagnosed at about age 31, after having experienced symptoms for about a year. Her treatment, if any, is unknown. Brenda's grandfather (age 74) has a history of bipolar disorder, type 1. He first had symptoms at age 16 and was diagnosed at age 26. He has been hospitalized twice, but is currently doing well with lithium.

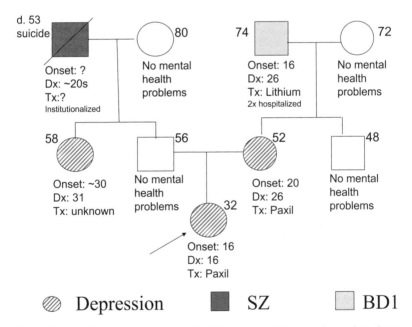

Figure 3.2. Pedigree showing a family history in which several members have mental illness. Each diagnosis is indicated by a different style of shading. For each affected individual, age at onset, age at diagnosis, and treatment is indicated beneath their symbol. Ages of each individual are indicated in an upper corner of their pedigree symbol. The index case (the client from whom the history is being taken) is indicated by means of the arrow.

Brenda's grandfather received a diagnosis of schizophrenia in his 20s, was institutionalized, and died by suicide in his 50s. There are no other affected family members.

Family History Documentation Method 2: Pedigree

In Figure 3.2, the same family history described in method 1 (narrative form) is drawn as a standardized pedigree, using the techniques described above and illustrated in Figure 3.1.

Comparison of the Two Methods

Although all of the information about affected family members is included in the written description, it often is more difficult to discern biological relationships—for example, which affected grandfather is related to Brenda through her mother, and which is related to her through her father, and whether her aunt with depression is related through her mother or father. Further, it is not clear whether there are unaffected family members. The narrative method requires careful reading in order to piece together the information to generate a holistic impression of the significance of the family history, whereas the pedigree allows very rapid identification of number/proportion of affected family members and the types of diagnosis.

Definitions and Concepts

A specific language is often applied to the family history information. In the following material, we provide definitions/descriptions of the most commonly used terms and phrases.

Degrees of relationship: First-degree relatives are children, siblings, and parents. Second-degree relatives are half-siblings, aunts, uncles, nieces, nephews, grandparents, and grandchildren. Third-degree relatives are first cousins, great-grandchildren and great-grandparents. (See Figure 3.3.)

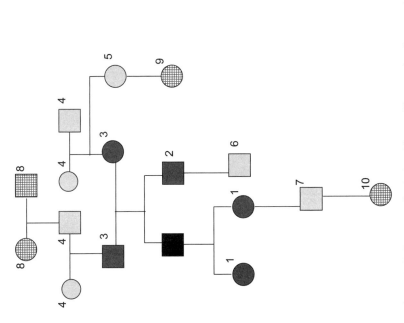

Legend

■ Index individual

● First degree relative

□ Second degree relative

▦ Third degree relative

Relationship to index individual:

1: Children   7: Grandchild

2: Sibling   8: Great grandparent

3: Parents   9: Cousin

4: Grandparents   10: Great grandchild

5: Aunt

6: Nephew

Figure 3.3. Degrees of relationship are illustrated using standardized pedigree format. Different degrees of relationship are indicated by means of different shading.

"Targeted" versus "comprehensive" family history: Genetics professionals use the term *targeted* to describe a family history specifically directed toward identifying risk for one particular disorder or class of disorders. In contrast, a comprehensive family history is taken to identify increased risk for *any* type of medical disorder. As a mental health clinician, it is beyond your mandate to identify increased risk for any type of medical disorder, so the information provided in this chapter aims to help clinicians gather a family history that is targeted toward psychiatric illnesses.

"Positive" and "negative" family histories: A family history is termed *positive* when the disorder(s) in question is identified in one or more relative. A *negative* history is one in which no disorder(s) in question is reported in the family. In this case, *negative* signals good news in terms of family risk.

What about Environmental Exposures in the Family History?

We have focused on the effects of both genetic and environmental factors in causing psychiatric disorders. What should you ask about environmental risk factors when you take a personal or family medical history? This is a difficult area because the meaning of a suspected environmental risk factor is difficult to interpret in any one client's personal or family history. You can ask about birth trauma or head injury, but it is difficult to "score" different sorts of birth traumas and head injuries in terms of psychiatric risk. You could ask about stress, but perception of stress is extremely personal, and "high" stress is difficult to define because of its subjective nature. In most cases, we do not know enough about the suspected link between psychiatric disease and viral exposure to ask useful questions. Use of cannabis or methamphetamine seems to be the most straightforward risk factor. In our practice, we do ask about specific environmental exposures and attempt to integrate the exposure information into our risk assessment and counseling. This is likely to be beyond the purview of most mental health clinicians, however.

One of the benefits of the family history is that it provides clues about genetic and environmental risk factors shared in the family, regardless of what the specific risk factors may be. A risk evaluation based on family history automatically captures some of the relevant environmental components.

Tips for Incorporating Family History Information into Practice

Risk assessment for psychiatric illness requires as complete a family history as possible, and personalized discussion of the causes of psychiatric illness is facilitated by a greater quantity of information. It is important to initiate the discussion of causes and degree of risk in a calm, comfortable location that is free of distractions. Similar to other therapeutic interactions, it is of course important to maintain confidentiality when discussing these topics; it can be easy to lose sight of the private and sensitive nature of family history data.

Some clients are eager and prepared to disclose and discuss their family medical history at the beginning of the risk counseling session. For those clients, after a brief discussion about the goals and outcome of the family history, we tend to initiate the history-taking process near the beginning of the session. We use the family history process as a way to learn more about the client, and we always incorporate education and psychosocial counseling into this phase. For clients who are less willing to share information, it may be best to begin the session with some education about causes of psychiatric illness and a careful discussion of how the family history may inform a more targeted discussion about those. From there, we may undertake some psychosocial counseling about the experience of living with psychiatric illness in the family. Generally the most relevant family history information comes out as part of this discussion. We then build upon this basic information to flesh out the family history, after the client feels more comfortable.

Collecting information about at least three generations of biological relations is standard, but it is beneficial to collect as much information as possible. The fact that both genetics and environment are involved in contributing to the development of psychiatric illness means that the disorders cluster in families, instead of segregating in a predictable fashion. So, unaffected relatives can, and will, pass susceptibility genes to children (see Chapter 4 for further discussion), which makes it important to obtain information about close relatives of unaffected family members as well as those of affected family members. When collecting the family history data, consider the following:

- *Begin with the client and his/her first-degree relatives* (see definition above) and then work up to the next generation and out to more distant relatives. For example, you could ask about the client's siblings, then children, then parents, then grandparents, then uncles and aunts, and then cousins.
- *Ask about the age at onset, illness course, and treatment for anyone in the family with a psychiatric illness.* These factors can inform the personalized discussion of the causes of psychiatric illness (as is detailed in Chapter 4) and the risk assessment (as is detailed in Chapter 5).
- *Don't just ask about psychiatric diagnoses.* Instead, ask about mental health in general, for example, whether people have taken medications for their mood or "nerves." Sometimes a client does not know if a particular relative ever received a psychiatric diagnosis, but then describes that relative as having strange beliefs or behaviors (e.g., "He was such a loner," or "The things that she believed were often really bizarre"). In such a case it can be useful to ask about developmental history (e.g., has the individual achieved normal milestones for age, such as independent living and employment?) and social relationships (e.g., does the individual have any close relationships?). If your clinical experience leads you to suspect a symptomatic relative based on information you obtain during the

family history process, it can be helpful to work through the most likely scenario: that the person (1) has not been diagnosed because he or she has not sought treatment; (2) did not meet full criteria for a psychiatric disorder but has symptoms related to the disorder in the family; or (3) has been diagnosed but not shared this with the family. Ideally, such relatives should undergo a psychiatric evaluation, though it is likely that most will decline.

• *Ask about suicide and suicide attempts,* which are, of course, very common in each of the major psychiatric illnesses, and conversely, psychiatric illnesses are very common in those who commit suicide. It is especially important to discuss suicide risk with clients who have a strong family history of suicide. There seem to be independent risk factors for suicide that make it more likely that a person will attempt or commit suicide if he of she has a family history of suicide.

• *Ask about substance misuse.* Substance misuse is a serious psychiatric issue in its own right and should be documented in the family history and addressed with clients. Also keep in mind the high rates of comorbidity between the major psychiatric illnesses and substance misuse.

• *Gather information about family members of all ages,* including young people in addition to adults. If the disorder of specific concern to your client is a psychiatric illness that typically has a childhood onset, the rationale for collecting information about young people in the family is clear. It is equally important to ask about young people in the family if the disorder of concern typically is of adult onset, however. For example, if the concern is bipolar disorder, which typically has onset in adolescence or 20s, collecting information about the presence or absence of attention-deficit hyperactivity disorder (ADHD) in younger family members can be important, as it may indicate increased familial risk (Birmaher et al., 2010).

• *Let the disorder in question guide the focus and the depth of the information* elicited about generations above and below the client's, but keep in mind that clues may be found in unexpected places. Anticipate that clients will know less about relatives as they become more distantly related. If clients do have information about more distant relatives, be aware that diagnoses may be less reliable and that histories of "institutionalizations" and "nervous breakdowns" must be interpreted in light of the social context of the time.

- *Collect family history from both the maternal and paternal sides of the family.* This is important for two reasons. First, psychiatric diagnoses are very common, and it is not unusual to find cases on both sides of the family history. Second, assortative mating (the tendency of individuals with a certain characteristic to have children with another person with the same characteristic) is not uncommon in populations with psychiatric illness (Merikangas, 1982).

- *Focus on biological relatives when taking the family history.* Help clients appreciate the importance of focusing on information about "blood" relatives. Nevertheless, clients may have family stories to impart that center on nonbiological relatives (e.g., stepparents, stepsiblings, uncles or aunts by marriage) and that are important to a full understanding of family relationships and your client's environment. But it is important both for risk assessment and for personalizing your discussion of causes of psychiatric illness to be certain about which relatives are "blood" relations, and which are not. Thus, it is important to clarify relationships, for example, by asking, "Do all of your brothers and sisters share the same mother and father?" This question helps to distinguish between full siblings (first-degree relatives), half siblings (second-degree relatives), and adopted siblings (usually nonbiological relations). Also be sure to ask whether aunts, uncles, cousins, etc., are related through the client's mother or father, since this detail becomes important for risk assessment.

How to Gather a Psychiatric Family History: Seven Easy Steps!

Information gathering usually begins with the client and proceeds to first-degree relatives, then second-degree relatives and third-degree relatives—and further, if possible. Remember to ask about both maternal and paternal relatives.

1. Document ages for all relatives included in the family history. Include affected and unaffected family members, because both are important for risk assessment.
2. Identify any individuals diagnosed with any psychiatric illness, whether childhood, adult, postpartum, or geriatric onset. Document diagnosis, age at diagnosis, and age at symptom onset. Do not limit yourself to asking about only one diagnosis or you might miss comorbid or co-occurring psychiatric illnesses in the client or family members. Ask about the mental health history of both living and deceased relatives.
3. Identify any individuals who are reported to be symptomatic of a psychiatric illness and those who have been treated for psychiatric symptoms or take a psychotropic medication, even if they are undiagnosed or the diagnosis is not known. Ask about relatives with very unusual behaviors or interpersonal skills.
4. Ask about death by suicide or suicidal ideation or attempts.
5. Ask about individuals who have problems with drug or alcohol misuse.
6. Document birth defects, mental retardation or learning disabilities, and unusual medical conditions.
7. Date and sign the family history data.

Confirming Diagnoses

In the majority of our cases, we have not been able to obtain medical records or undertake a psychiatric evaluation of a symptomatic relative. In these cases, we find it useful to get as much information from the client as possible and to use the family history to help guide our judgment. We take advantage of our knowledge that particular groups of disorders are more likely to cluster in families. Though this approach can be tricky and is never an appropriate way to diagnose a disorder, for the sake of risk assessment, we may assume that a symptomatic and undiagnosed relative has a disorder that fits within the spectrum of disorders that appears in the family. If the relative's reported symptoms do not fit within the spectrum, we then consider the possibility that there are two different sets of disorders clustering in the family.

We always take care to document which individuals are reported to have been diagnosed and differentiate them from those who are reported as symptomatic. We categorize information based on what is known (a verified diagnosis in a relative; the diagnosis in our own client), what is likely (a diagnosis reported by a client who has no reason not to be a reasonable informant), and what is suspected or possible (a related diagnosis in a relative who is reported as symptomatic but is undiagnosed; a possible diagnosis in a relative based on treatments used). When it comes time to use the pedigree to evaluate the pattern in the family and to inform risk assessment, we consider alternate scenarios that include risk with and without those probable and possible individuals as affected.

How Long Does It Take to Gather a Targeted Psychiatric Family History?

We expect that you might, understandably, have concerns about the time it will take to collect a targeted psychiatric family history. We encourage you to try different collection methods and find which works best for you. People are often surprised by how quickly they can obtain the information, especially after some practice. Initial collection of family history data for a new client can usually be done in about 10 minutes for most families, even those with a fairly significant illness load in the family—though you are likely to find that many clients are eager to engage in a compressive discussion of their family history and their lived family experience, and often will extend the discussion significantly if you are able and willing to take advantage of this rich moment for learning about the client and building rapport. The family history can be updated over regular intervals and never needs to be completely redone. For those clients with whom you already have the benefit of an established relationship, family history data collection and counseling about causes of psychiatric illness and family risk can be integrated over a series of visits, and may not even necessitate an additional visit.

Barriers to Gathering a Psychiatric Family History

The primary challenges to taking a psychiatric family history are the diagnostic uncertainty related to the disorders and the large percentage of affected individuals who have not been diagnosed or treated. In addition to the inherent issues related to clinical diagnoses, the features of illness tend to change over time and can be clouded by comorbidity. Other important barriers include the following factors:

- The stigma related to psychiatric illness might make an individual reluctant or unwilling to share a personal or family history.
- Families tend to hide a history of psychiatric illness, and the client may not be aware of affected individuals or may not know their current diagnosis.
- Clients or family members might describe their illness with a more socially accepted diagnosis that is perceived as less severe.
- Highly symptomatic clients might have find it difficult or be unwilling to provide family history information.

• Because of their illness, individuals with psychiatric diagnoses may be more likely to be alienated from their families and have less information.

We have found that some clients are only willing to provide all of the information that they know about their own psychiatric history and that of family members after they feel comfortable with the goals, process, and outcome of the targeted psychiatric history. It is common for clients to recall additional information as they begin to see how we use their information to evaluate risk; that is, they begin to realize which information is most relevant and may provide additional details. It is also not uncommon for clients to choose not to provide some information that they perceive as more private until they get a better understanding of the process and more comfortable with us. We make it a habit to check in with the client at the end of the family history as we enter the risk communication process to see if he or she has recalled or is now willing to share any additional information.

Accuracy of Self-Reported Family History

From the perspective of providing the most comprehensive assessment of risk, in a perfect situation, you would obtain medical records for all affected relatives to confirm the diagnoses and gather additional details, such as diagnostic history and age at onset and diagnosis. In addition, any family members reported as potentially symptomatic, but undiagnosed, would undergo a psychiatric evaluation. Realistically, however, clients are often reluctant to approach family members to obtain consent for the release of records or to suggest a psychiatric evaluation. Even if the client requests it of his or her relatives, the affected family members (especially when symptomatic) may not agree to release records.

Studies evaluating the accuracy of self-reported psychiatric family history suggest that this method of information gathering has moderate to good sensitivity (wherein individuals reported as affected are correctly identified) and very good specificity (wherein individuals in the family who are not affected are correctly reported as such) (Weissman et al., 2000). The accuracy of the family history may depend on many factors, including whether the informant is affected (and if so, with what disorder), about what disorder information is being provided, and how many informants provide information (Chapman et al., 1994; Weissman et al., 2000). Research suggests that, if error exists, it is likely to be an underestimation of the family load of psychiatric illness. It seems that family history is more accurate for more severe disorders (e.g., schizophrenia) than for less severe disorders (e.g., anxiety disorders) (Milne et al., 2009). It is important that clients understand that risk assessment information relies on the *assumed diagnosis of relatives*. When records are not available or when the diagnosis is uncertain, risk assessment relies completely on the client's self-reported history. The risk assessment provided is only as good as the information the client reports, and the clinician must ensure that the client is clear about this caveat.

You can potentially increase the accuracy of family history by taking advantage of the following tips:

- In advance of the visit, provide the client with a list of the questions that you will ask so that he or she can gather information.
- Encourage the client to approach affected relatives, older relatives, and/or the family historian to obtain information.
- If the client is acutely symptomatic or known to be a poor historian, request that a relative provide family history data.
- Ask about all relatives individually or in small groups. For example, instead of saying, "Do you have any cousins with any mental health concerns?" ask "Your Aunt Rosa—did she have any children? And were there any concerns in any of her children? And Uncle Jose, did he have children? Did any of his children have psychiatric illnesses or symptoms?" Ask about the health of closer relatives, such as siblings, individually.

What to Expect from a Targeted Psychiatric Family History

The majority of individuals with psychiatric illnesses have few or no affected relatives. Although this may seem counterintuitive for a condition where genetics is an important contributor to illness development, it is typical of all common, complex disorders. While only few of your clients will have complicated, "positive," or "loaded" family histories, keep in mind that even having one first-degree relative with a major psychiatric disorder is the largest known risk factor for disorder onset. In other words, your client's children, siblings, and parents are (empirically) already in the highest known risk category for illness onset that is possible for asymptomatic individuals. In addition, a negative family history provides as much information about risk as does a positive family history. Knowing that other relatives are not affected lets you more confidently use empirical risks to estimate the magnitude of risk (see Chapter 5).

What You Can Say to Clients and Family Members When Gathering the Family History

"I'm going to ask you questions about your family members' mental health, in general how they are doing, and whether they have any serious medical issues or birth defects with which they were born. This family history information will help me to explain to you what caused the psychiatric illness in your family, and what the chances are that other people in your family might develop psychiatric illness, too."

Explaining the process and the purpose up front is a good idea. It is also usually very well received if you show the developing family history document to your client during the process. It is also usually appreciated if you provide your client with an estimate of how long the family history-taking process will last; explain that how much time it takes varies depending on how large the client's family is and how much information he or she has about family members, but that it usually does not take more than 10–15 minutes.

"Don't worry if you don't know about the mental health status of all of your family members. I understand that many families tend not to talk about psychiatric illnesses. Would you feel comfortable to approach your family to find out more?"

Clients can sometimes get anxious if they feel that you are asking a lot of questions that they cannot answer. Particularly if they are very anxious about having a risk assessment, not being able to fully answer these questions can feel like failure. In such situations, you can use statements like those above to attempt to alleviate that worry. If you already have a well-established relationship with the client, you may already know whether he or she would feel comfortable approaching family members for additional information, or if the individual cannot get more information (because the family member is deceased), or would rather not ask (because of poor relationships or because the relatives do not know of the client's diagnosis). Reassure such clients with a statement like, "No problem, we can work with what you do know."

"This family history is generated from information you provided, but I wonder what your perspective is on it now that you are seeing it laid out like this—how are you feeling about it?"

Even though the family history is generated using information provided by the client, sometimes seeing it clearly laid out can be quite startling. This may be particularly true when individuals who have mental illnesses are highlighted. While many clients have previously thought about the mental health of relatives, they may not have done so in a systematic way, with a goal of identifying areas of genetic overlap between diagnoses in the family. Seeing the graphic presentation of the family history may bring the client to a more concrete realization of his or her personal or family risks. This provides a key teachable moment that should not be missed, but you should pay attention to the client's affect throughout the process.

Issues That Clients and Their Families May Raise

"Why do you want to know about how old everyone was when they first got sick?"

You can respond to such a question by acknowledging that it may seem odd or irrelevant to ask these sorts of questions, but that this kind of information can be useful in approximating what might have caused the illness in the family member, and in helping you to provide them with the best information that you can about risks that relatives might be similarly affected.

"No, no one else in my family had psychosis . . . well, I guess my brother did, but he was taking drugs when it happened, so it's not related to my diagnosis."

This kind of statement is actually very helpful because it provides some insight into how this client perceives his brother's illness experience as arising from a very different set of contributing factors from his own. It would be important for you to ask some follow-up questions, such as about the type of drug the brother used at the time of the psychosis and for how long the psychosis lasted. You should note the brother's history in the family history data, and explain to the client that it is hard to say for certain whether that history is related to the client's own diagnosis.

"Can I see what you are writing about my family history?"

Clients are often very interested in seeing the compiled information about their family histories. Especially if you take the family history in a pedigree format, clients may ask to have copies of the information to bring home. We always encourage this curiosity and show clients the developing pedigree and explain what the symbols mean. Developing the family history collaboratively is an excellent rapport-building tool, and helps to engage clients fully in the process.

Our Experience

Case Example

Joann was a 22-year-old woman with a diagnosis of unipolar major depression. She recently became engaged, and her engagement caused her to think more about the cause and likely trajectory of her illness, as well as her potential to have children with a mood disorder. After some discussion about the goals of the counseling session, I (HP) described the importance of the family history. Joann explained to me that she thought that mood disorders were common in her family, but that her relatives were extremely unwilling to discuss mental illness. She therefore asked her mother whether she could share any information she knew about mood illness in the family. Joann and her mother engaged in their first frank discussion about Joann's illness and the history in the family, and Joann's mother admitted that she had been treated for years for depression herself—this was the first time that Joann learned of her mother's mood disorder. Joann's mother also shared the limited information she had obtained through rumors she'd heard about other relatives' illnesses. Joann perceived this information sharing as a major gift that her mother had given to her. Joann and I spent some time discussing what it was like living in a family with so much secrecy, and what it was like to learn about her mother's illness. I used the available family history information and Joann's medical history to provide the best assessment of etiology and risk possible. Joann asked if I would summarize the information in a letter, because she felt strongly about sharing it with her relatives in an effort to reduce the secrecy and stigma in her family.

Case Example

Takia was a 27-year-old pregnant woman who was referred by her psychiatrist to consult with me (JA) because of concerns related to taking a mood stabilizer during pregnancy. She was interested in advice about whether to discontinue the medication during pregnancy, and about how she might reduce the teratogenic potential if she remained on the medication. She seemed quite uncomfortable at the beginning of the session. Contracting about the goals of the session was helpful, but when I mentioned that I would ask for family history information, she emotionally disconnected from our interaction. Noting her response, I shifted the focus and spent quite a while talking about her hopes for her baby and concerns about the medication use versus the potential for her symptoms to increase if she stopped the medication. After a thorough discussion of teratogenic risks, I again brought up the possibility of gathering a family history so that I could provide her with more information about etiology and risk. At this point, we had established a good rapport. She was willing to open up to me and told a dramatic story of generations of illness and the effect of the illness on her childhood years. As the session continued, she continued to add additional details to the family history. I ended up with a very comprehensive family history that I would not have obtained if I had not been responsive to the client's need for rapport before sharing what she considered to be very sensitive information.

PART II

TALKING WITH FAMILIES

Deeper Discussions

CHAPTER FOUR

Explaining How Psychiatric Illness Happens

In this chapter we present strategies for understanding and discussing the environmental contributions to psychiatric illness and their complicated interactions with each other as well as with genetic factors. We provide tools and suggestions for presenting the concept that genes and environment work together to contribute to psychiatric illnesses.

Nature or Nurture?

For many years the causes of psychiatric illnesses were subjects of heated debate among interested health-care professionals and academics. In general, those with biomedical training in mental health tended to favor explanations for the origins of psychiatric illness that emphasized biological mechanisms (a medical model), whereas those with training in the humanities tended to favor explanations that emphasized experiences and environment (a social model). The popular press fueled the debate, framing news stories about the origins of psychiatric illness as questions about whether these illnesses are caused by "nature or nurture."

In recent years the debate around the subject has subsided considerably, because across professionals with disparate training backgrounds a general consensus of opinion has been reached about the origins of psychiatric illness. There is now widespread support for the idea that psychiatric illnesses are typically caused by neither "nature" nor "nurture" alone, but rather, like other common disorders (cancer, heart disease, etc.), they arise as a result of combined influence of both biological (nature) and environmental (nurture) contributions (McClearn, 2004). The renowned psychologist Donald Hebb was credited with describing this concept with an effective analogy. In response to a question about whether "nature or nurture" was more important in molding behavior, he pointed out that all aspects of behavior are jointly determined by heredity and environment, in much the same way as the area of a rectangle is jointly determined by its length and width.

This same analogy can be applied to the question of whether nature or nurture is more important in the development of psychiatric illness: In the vast majority of cases, both contribute to the to the cause. Thus, although different disciplines use different terminology to describe the cause of psychiatric illness (e.g., the stress–vulnerability–competence model, stress diathesis, chemical imbalance), the underlying concept that was so evocatively articulated by Hebb is now, by and large, common to all. It is interesting to consider the causes of psychiatric illness in light of accepted treatment strategies for these conditions. Specifically, treatment for psychiatric illness tends to fall into one of two categories: biological (pharmacological) and/or psychosocial. It would seem fitting and appropriate that the models used to explain the pathogenesis of these illnesses should reflect the concepts underlying their efficacious treatment.

Although there are scientific data to support the idea that psychiatric illnesses are typically caused by the combined influences of both genetic and environmental contributions (Cardno et al., 1999; Cooper, 2001), much remains to be clarified. The complete set of genetic factors that contributes to psychiatric illness remain to be identified, as do many of the environmental factors, and the complexity of the range of potential interactions between different combinations of these is only beginning to be appreciated. Although the interplay between genes and environment is extremely complex, research is beginning to elucidate some of the specific mechanisms that are involved in psychiatric illness.

Conceptually, it is important to appreciate that neither genes nor environment exist in the absence of the other, and that interaction between the two can potentially occur in a number of different ways. First, our genes influence the way that we respond to different types of environments. For example, based on a person's genetic variations he or she might be more vulnerable to psychiatric illness after using cannabis than someone with different genetic variations (Caspi et al., 2005). We know that environmental effects can modify genes; for example, there is evidence that high levels of stress can cause differences in the amount of protein produced by some genes (Ni et al., 1999) (if you remember from Chapter 1, the amount of protein produced by a given gene is regulated, in part, by a process called methylation); thus, high levels of stress can cause changes in production levels of different brain chemicals. Second, genotype may affect the types of environments to which an individual exposes him- or herself; for example, certain genetic variations may predispose individuals to seek out and engage in risky activities (Lin et al., 2005; Kreek et al., 2005).

Another important concept is that sets of genetic risk factors interact with one another, just as different environmental risk factors interact with one another (Tandon et al., 2008). Risk genes interact with each other in complicated ways that, in terms of resulting risk, may be addititive, multiplicative, or exponential. There are also likely to be protective genetic variants that reduce risk. The same is true of environmental factors; it is easy to imagine that, for example, a stressful life experience in someone who has had adequate sleep and exercise might cause a very different biochemical response than one in someone who is sleep- and exercise-deprived. New research technologies and new ways of conceptualizing the complexity of the underlying causes of psychiatric illness provide promise that the coming years will herald continued progress in our understanding (Williams, 2009). Before we discuss how genes and enviroment interact in the development of psychiatric illnesses, we first discuss what is known about environmental contributors to psychiatric illness.

Environmental Factors That Contribute to Psychiatric Illness

In the context of discussing the factors that contribute to illness (and indeed, to the large majority of human traits), "environment" has a very broad meaning. Environmental factors include anything outside of the genome that can affect the expression of a gene, including the in utero environment, shared and nonshared home environments, type and quality of social interactions and experiences, exposures to harmful substances, and medical treatment. The same data from twin studies that were useful in demonstrating that genes play an important role in the development of psychiatric illness also show that genes are not the only contributors. As we saw in Chapter 1, the "concordance rates" for psychiatric illnesses in identical (monozygotic, or MZ) twins is always less than 100% (Cardno et al., 1999; Smoller & Finn, 2003), and therefore we can conclude that there is an important environmental influence in the development of these illnesses.

Environmental factors act on gene expression throughout the lifetime, from preconception until death. Based on any individual's genes, he or she might not react to a particular environmental factor at all, or the environmental factor might be beneficial or protective, or the environmental factor might be harmful. To add further complexity, these effects might be different at different times in a person's life—that is, something that is harmful in infancy might be neutral in later childhood and protective as an adult.

Many families have an intuitive understanding that personal experiences, or "environment," can contribute to the development of a psychiatric illness. For example, a stressful event of some kind often precedes an episode of anxiety, depression, mania, or psychosis, and affected individuals and their families frequently notice this temporal connection. Other families may note the association between substance use and the onset of psychiatric symptoms or may perceive that a difficult home environment played a role in illness onset.

Families and clinicians naturally (and correctly) have a high level of interest in environmental risk factors for psychiatric disorders. In theory, at least some aspects of environment are controllable and modifiable, and there are both risk-increasing and protective environmental factors. This means that, if we are able to identify and modify risk factors, it would be possible to reduce the risk for psychiatric illness in at-risk individuals. Unfortunately, we anticipate continued difficulty with unequivocally identifying the particular environmental factors that could be used to inform risk management strategies at the level of the individual because research is necessarily population based. However, clients can often identify quite clearly environmental factors that can *trigger* an episode of illness for them (e.g., stress at work combined with poor sleep). So investigating these factors can offer important elements of control for clients and families.

Overall, research to date has provided strong support for both genetic and environmental risk factors as contributing to the development of major psychiatric disorders. This large research base leads us to believe that most individuals with psychiatric illnesses have experienced one or more environmental risk factors that contributed to their illness. But it seems that, in the large majority of cases, those environmental factors were not sufficient to cause the disorder by themselves. Rather, the environmental risk factors acted together with genetic risk factors to cause illness.

Research provides us with some information about what types of environmental risk are most important. For most major psychiatric illnesses of adult onset, studies indicate that nonshared environmental risk factors are more important in contributing to the development of psychiatric illness than are shared environmental factors (Hicks et al., 2009; Kendler & Prescott, 1999; Tsuang, Stone & Faraone, 2001).

Shared environmental risk factors are those to which more than one member of the family is exposed. Nonshared environmental risk factors are unique to individual family members (e.g., substance abuse). A common misconception is that parenting and home environment are always environmental factors shared by siblings. This is not necessarily true; parenting style often differs for siblings based on parent and child factors, and the home environment might change considerably over time. In addition, related to psychiatric illnesses, it is often the individual's *perception* of his or her parenting and home environment that is likely important to mental well-being and psychiatric illness. Therefore, even if siblings experienced identical parenting and home environment, we would not anticipate that the two siblings would *experience* the parenting and the home environment in the same way. This is because the siblings have different personality types and respond differently to identical stimuli—and these differences are likely to be related to the siblings' genes.

The compexity of these variations raises one last important point about environmental risk factors. Many of the "environmental" factors that play a role in psychiatric illness are themselves driven by a small, moderate, or large genetic component. For example, substance use is an environmental risk factor, but there are also genetic factors that influence how likely individuals are to use and misuse drugs (Philbert et al., 2009).

Some of the environmental factors that have been implicated in the development of psychiatric illness are described below; we focus primarily on schizophrenia, for which most data exist. The environmental factors identified to date are primarily factors that increase risk, but you should keep in mind that there are protective environmental factors as well. This list is not exhaustive, and knowledge in this area is still emerging.

Stress

Although a stressful event of some kind often precedes an episode of psychiatric illness, and is often described by families as the "trigger" for illness onset, it is difficult to define and quantify stress. Major events such as the death of a loved one, a relationship breakup, traumatic experiences such as a car crash, and financial or work-related crises can certainly be important contributors in the development of a psychiatric illness—though illness-triggering events are not always so recognizable to the observer. Less obvious events that the individual appraises to be stressful can also be important in illness onset. Stress seems to directly influence how genes instruct the body about how to grow, develop, and function, especially in individuals with certain genotypes. Stress has been shown to affect the brain by influencing genes, which in turn cause variation in the amounts of certain brain chemicals (Ni et al., 1999). It is thought that stress could influence risk for psychiatric illness through this mechanism.

Drug Use

Certain drugs appear to contribute to the development of some kinds of psychiatric illness, particularly psychotic disorders, in individuals who are genetically vulnerable. In particular, crystal methamphetamine can trigger psychosis that persists even after the drug has cleared from the system (Grelotti et al., 2010), and so is of particular concern in terms of use by already-vulnerable individuals. When used in adolescence, cannabis also seems to increase the risk in genetically vulnerable individuals for psychosis in later life (Degenhardt et al., 2003). People with existing psychiatric illness who use cannabis have poorer outcome than those who do not use cannabis (Degenhardt et al., 2003). Drugs such as cannabis and methamphetamine may increase risk for psychiatric illness by directly influencing the quantities of certain brain chemicals.

Paternal Age

One of the most well-replicated findings of contributors to psychiatric disorders is that paternal age at the time of conception is related to risk for offspring to develop schizophrenia (Torrey et al., 2009). Similar findings are emerging for bipolar disorder (Menezes et al., 2010) and autism (Reichenberg et al., 2006). The highest risks to offspring are seen for those whose fathers were 55 or older at the time of conception. When fathers are more than 55 years old at the time of conception, the risk seems to double (to about a 2% risk) as compared to the risk for offspring of fathers in the youngest age category (about a 1% risk) (Zammit et al., 2003). Although the mechanism by which paternal age affects offspring risk for psychiatric illness is not known with certainty, we do know that the chance for spontaneous genetic variation in sperm increases as men get older; thus, it is possible that paternal age influences offspring risk for psychiatric illness because the chance that variations will occur in associated risk genes also increases (Reichenberg et al., 2006).

Obstetric Complications

Complications of both pregnancy (e.g., preeclampsia, diabetes, rhesus incompatibility) and delivery (e.g., lack of oxygen during delivery and emergency caesarian section) are associated with increased risk for a newborn to develop schizophrenia in later life. Individuals whose perinatal period was complicated are two to four times more likely to develop schizophrenia than those whose perinatal period was not complicated (Cannon et al., 2002). The evidence regarding risk for mood disorders associated with obstetric complications is less clear, but there is some evidence that children who were born prematurely may have somewhat increased risk (Laursen et al., 2007). The exact mechanisms by which obstetric complications increase risk for psychiatric illness are not understood.

Season of Birth

There seems to be a small but significant increase in the rate of schizophrenia among individuals born in the winter or spring as compared to those who were born in the summer or fall (Torrey et al., 1997). The data for the Northern Hemisphere are stronger than those for the Southern Hemisphere. Some evidence seems to support similar trends for mood disorders (Torrey et al., 1997). The mechanisms behind this association are not well understood, but some researchers have hypothesized that increased frequency, or specific types, of infection or low prenatal levels of vitamin D in the winter/spring months as compared to the summer/fall may contribute to the risk.

Head Injury

For individuals who are genetically vulnerable, sustaining a head injury seems to increase risk for schizophrenia (Kim, 2008), and there is some evidence that a similar trend may exist for mood disorders (Jorge & Robinson, 2003). Again, the mechanism by which head injuries contribute to risk for psychiatric illness is not well understood.

Urban Upbringing

There is good evidence that urban birth or urban upbringing is associated with an increased risk for schizophrenia (Pedersen & Mortenson, 2001). Although there are many theories regarding why this might be (including increased frequency of infection and higher levels of pollutants and stress in urban areas), there are no conclusive data. Only scant research has been conducted with the aim of investigating the relationship between urban upbringing and mood disorders.

Immigration

There is evidence that both first- and second-generation immigrants have increased risks for schizophrenia (Hutchinson & Haasen, 2004). There are few data and inconclusive evidence regarding the relationship between mood disorders and immigration. With respect to schizophrenia, researchers have effectively controlled for many potential confounders in the studies investigating this issue, and one of the most interesting theories about the mechanism by which the risk is increased relates to the effects of the social adversity often faced by immigrants.

Maternal Famine

Exposure to famine during pregnancy has been shown to increase the risk for the offspring to develop psychiatric illnesses, including major mood disorders or schizophrenia, later in life (Hoek et al., 1998). The reduced availability of vital nutrients is thought to be responsible for this increased risk.

Infection

There has been considerable interest in the question of whether infection with viral or other agents (e.g., parasites such as toxoplasmosis) can contribute to risk for psychiatric illness. The results generated to date have not demonstrated that infection is a major contributor to risk (Brown & Derkits, 2010; Dalman et al., 2008).

Summary of Key Concepts
in the Cause of Psychiatric Illness

- There is significant heterogeneity of illness causes, features, and outcomes within diagnostic categories.
- There is no single factor that is "the risk factor" for any psychiatric illness.
- Many, if not all, of the risk factors for psychiatric illness increase risk for more than one disorder.
- Disorder onset usually requires an intersection of interacting genetic and environmental risk factors. There are differences among individuals in terms of the specific genetic and environmental factors that contribute to the development of the illness, and in the relative contributions of genes and environment.

Tips for Incorporating Information about Genetic and Environmental Contributions into Practice

Clients cannot achieve a holistic understanding of the causes of their illness without learning about the roles of both genetic and environmental factors. Although in our experience, clients' own intuitive attributions of cause tend to include both genes/biology and experiences, most express some uncertainty and confusion. Many clients have identified attributes in other relatives that make them more likely to become ill, including personality traits and environmental exposures. Conceptually, though, it can be quite difficult to get a solid grasp on exactly how genes and environment contribute together to the development of these illnesses. In our interactions with affected individuals and their families, we have used different techniques to convey the key concepts of this issue. In the paragraphs that follow, we present two complementary tools we have found to be most helpful in this regard: the jar model and the family history. When using these tools to discuss the roles of genes and environment, we try to incorporate clients' perceptions of environmental factors into the discussion. In Chapter 2 (Getting Started), we suggested that you consider asking questions such as, "Can you tell me a little about what was going on for you around the time that you first developed this illness?" This type of question can be a very effective way to identify environmental factors that a client perceives to have been significant in the onset of his or her illness, and it can be useful to refer back to any experiences that the client highlights while using these tools.

The Jar Model

Many people grasp concepts more easily when they are represented visually. We find a simple visual analogy very helpful in representing this difficult but important concept that genes and environment both contribute to psychiatric illness. The general concept in this model is that we all have a "mental illness jar," representing an overall risk for mental illness, and that the jar has to be filled to the top in order for the person to experience an active episode of illness. Two different kinds of factors go inside the jar: genetic and environmental. We represent the two kinds of factors with different colored and shaped objects. You can use a visual representation of the jar or a physical jar in your demonstrations. The jar analogy can present both vulnerability and protective factors very concretely. While the amount of genetic vulnerability in a jar remains constant, environmental vulnerability factors can be added to the jar as well as removed. A third element in the jar model is the protective factor; we use examples of medication and good social support network as protective factors that restrict access of environmental vulnerability factors to the jar. While it is a simple analogy, it accurately captures the core issues, in such a way that it can be used to help even those who might have cognitive difficulties to get a better understanding of the factors that contribute to illness, but it can also be used as a basis for more in-depth discussions for those with more sophisticated understanding. Thus, it can be used to meet the needs of a huge range of clients (see Figure 4.1).

Figure 4.1. The "mental illness jar," filled by two kinds of vulnerability factors.

The Family History

The psychiatric family history, as detailed in Chapter 3, can be very useful in illustrating the complex contributions of factors to the development of psychiatric illness in a very personal—and therefore powerful—way. Graphic pedigree representations of the family history are, by far, the most effective way to use the family history as a teaching tool. In the family histories of the large proportion of affected individuals who have no affected family members, you can describe how multiple risk factors had to come together to produce the illness. No one else in the family had sufficient risk factors to cause illness, but it is likely that there are genetic vulnerability factors that the client inherited from both sides of the family. If relevant to the client's needs, you can use the pedigree to illustrate the discussion about how an affected individual can pass genetic vulnerability to children. In addition, gathering information about life events that occurred around the time of illness onset for affected individuals can be a useful way to illustrate the role of environmental factors.

With an affected individual who has family members who had other psychiatric diagnoses, symptoms, or questionable histories, you can use the pedigree to illustrate the clustering that occurs in families and the shared genetic vulnerability to mental illness in biological relatives. In less common situations where the client has a complicated multigenerational pedigree or one in which there are many affected individuals in the same generation, you can use the pedigree to show how genetic vulnerability factors have been transmitted from generation to generation, or how risk factors have clustered into one generation and that the genetic vulnerability can be passed to subsequent generations. In Figure 4.2 we show an example of the sort of family history you might commonly encounter, in the format of a simplified (i.e., no ages of onset or treatment data are shown) pedigree.

You may find that using the family history and the jar model together creates the most individually relevant and easily grasped explanation.

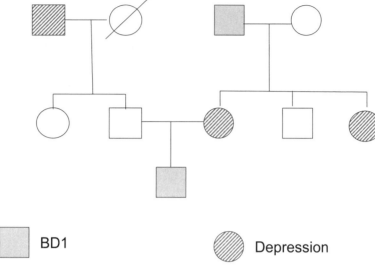

BD1   Depression

Figure 4.2. A typical psychiatric family history represented as a simplified pedigree; a pedigree like this can be used very effectively as a visual aid to personalize the discussion about the factors that can contribute to the development of mental illness.

What You Can Say to Clients and Family Members Using the Jar Model and Family History

We present below a similar group of questions as posed in Chapter 1, with more nuanced discussions that include the concept of genes and environment interacting to cause illness.

> *"It can be difficult to understand how genes and environment work together to cause the development of mental illness, so we can use this jar as a visual analogy to help you understand how mental illness arises. [See Figure 4.3.] Every one of us has a 'mental illness jar.' In order to have an active episode of mental illness, the jar has to be full. There are two different types of risk factors that can fill up our jars. The balls represent genetic risk factors, and the triangles represent environmental risk factors.*

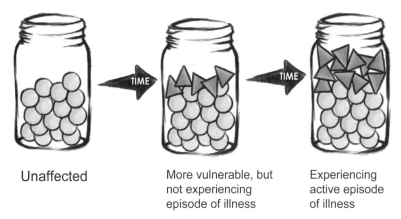

Unaffected   More vulnerable, but   Experiencing
                    not experiencing   active episode
                    episode of illness   of illness

Figure 4.3. The jar model can be used to show clients how mental illness can develop. Only when the jar is full to the top does an individual experience an active episode of illness. While the amount of genetic vulnerability stays constant, environmental vulnerability factors can accumulate over time.

Let's use this jar analogy to talk about how someone might develop mental illness, over time."

You can explain that the jar on the left represents how much genetic vulnerability, or risk, this individual inherited from his mom and dad, and that the jar is not full, so this individual is not experiencing an active episode of illness. Additional environmental factors may add up over time. Explain to your client that each of those experiences would perhaps add a few more environmental triangles to his jar, and at some point the jar becomes full, and the person then experiences an episode of illness. Note that it can be very effective to use plausible environmental vulnerability factors that the individual mentioned having experienced as examples of adding risk to the jar; take care, however, to debunk any incorrect beliefs about contributing factors (e.g., curses, bad character) that your client might have.

"The amount of genetic vulnerability in the jar stays the same over time."

Try to help clients understand that although the amount of environmental vulnerability in our jars can change over time, the amount of genetic vulnerability with which we are born stays the same.

"Different people will have different amounts of genetic vulnerability in their jars."

You could explain to your client that the person represented in the top row of Figure 4.4 has less genetic vulnerability in her jar and is less likely to develop mental illness (it is less likely that her jar will fill to the top, because there is more space in it), but the person represented in the bottom row is more likely to develop mental illness (there is only a small amount of space at the top of his jar, so it would take very little for it to fill up). If both people do go on to develop a mental illness, the person at the top is likely to be older than the individual at

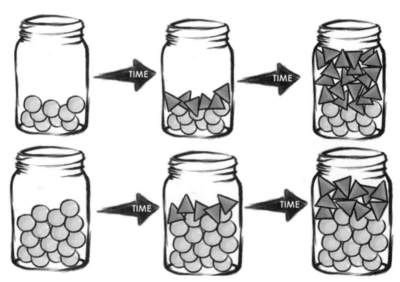

Figure 4.4. The jar model can be used to illustrate how different individuals will have different amounts of genetic vulnerability to mental illness. An alternate way to think about it is that the person at the top is "less sensitive" to her environment, and the person at the bottom is "more sensitive" to her environment.

the bottom when she first experiences an active episode of mental illness because it takes longer for her jar to fill up. You could then personalize the discussion by asking about your client's age at symptom onset and describing what this might indicate about his or her genetic vulnerability.

"We all have some amount of genetic vulnerability to a range of disorders, including psychiatric disorders and other types of disorders like heart disease and diabetes. Some of us will have very little genetic vulnerability, others of us will have a lot, but most of us likely have some intermediate amount."

You can use this discussion to directly challenge the idea that those with mental illness must be in some way biologically "different" or "other" than those who are not affected. We sometimes use the analogy of height to help clients understand the idea of population variability to genetic vulnerability. We talk about how a relatively small number of people will be shorter than 5'2, and similarly, relatively few will be taller than 6'2. Most people will fall somewhere in between. In the same way, it seems likely that while a few people will have either a very large amount or a very small amount of genetic vulnerability to mental illness, most will have some intermediate amount (see Figure 4.5).

You could also explain that it is not just those with mental illness who have genetic vulnerability. We can have a genetic vulnerability to mental illness but never get ill, because our experiences never cause the jar to fill to the top (see Figure 4.6). This is an important point that directly challenges any tendencies toward genetic fatalism an individual may have.

"It seems that what we inherit is a vulnerability to mental illness, rather than a vulnerability to [disorder X] specifically."

This is an important point. It is quite common to see family histories where there are multiple individuals each with a different mental illness. Research studies increasingly show that most genetic variants

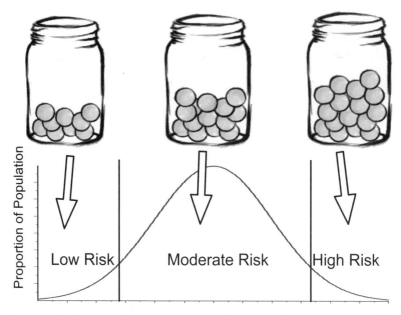

Figure 4.5. This kind of diagram can be used to help individuals with mental illness feel less "biologically different"—it depicts the idea that we all have some amount of genetic vulnerability to mental illness, and that within a population the amount of genetic vulnerability is normally distributed.

Figure 4.6. The jar model can be used to demonstrate that, even if someone has a lot of genetic vulnerability in their jar, it does not mean that it will necessarily fill up to the top. This point can be particularly helpful for affected individuals who are worried about their children.

that increase risk seem to increase vulnerability to mental illness (in a broadly defined way) rather than to a narrowly defined psychiatric diagnosis (Owen et al., 2007). Perhaps it is the individual combination of genetic and environmental contributors that determines whether an individual manifests bipolar disorder or schizophrenia, for example. You can tell the affected client that although he or she may have no family members with the exact same diagnosis, the family history of another diagnosis or group of diagnoses makes it is very likely that he or she inherited genetic vulnerability to mental illness in general.

"Some genes play an important role in how we respond to life events. Genetic variations in those genes may result in less than optimal response patterns in particular circumstances."

Help clients understand that one of the primary roles of genes is to respond to changes to the environment. Certain genetic variants seem to affect how individuals respond to particular environmental stimuli, such as drugs or stressful life events. To help the client understand this, you can ask him or her to think of friends and family members who bounce back easily from serious difficulties, and to think of others who are strongly affected by similar experiences. Genetic differences are part of the reason for this.

"Experiences/environmental factors do not usually cause psychiatric illness by themselves, but they can make a person more vulnerable to developing mental illness, or can 'trigger' an episode."

Clients or family members who attribute the development of a mental illness entirely to environmental factors may have increased perceptions of guilt or blame. Family members often feel guilty and blame themselves for their relative's mental illness. For example, parents of affected individuals may blame the appearance of the illness on their divorce or the fact that they had to move to a new home. Other families, especially those who have lived with the effects of mental illness for some time, will have heard the term or been exposed to the concept of the *schizophrenogenic mother* or other similar attributions of blame to members of the family. These blaming attributions often have a profoundly negative impact on a family, and learning that mental illness is not usually caused by environmental influences alone can be very helpful. It is also important to stress that many environmental influences are beyond a client's control. For affected individuals who attribute their illness to life choices such as their own substance use, understanding that such environmental factors usually do not cause illness by themselves can also help to alleviate debilitating guilt and self-blame.

Experiencing an active episode of illness

Vulnerable, but not actively ill

Less likely to relapse

Protective factor

Figure 4.7. We find it useful to talk about how mental illness develops before we talk about how people can recover from having an active episode of illness. In this diagram, although the amount of genetic vulnerability in the jar remains the same, some environmental factors are removed from the jar. We also introduce the concept of "protective factors" at this point. The idea with protective factors is that they do not function as a lid to the jar, rather they make the opening at the top of the jar narrower (thus harder for environmental factors to get back in), and/or you can talk about them as making the jar taller (and therefore more environmental factors are needed to fill it up again).

"We can also use this jar model to explain how people can recover from an active episode of illness."

It can be very helpful to understand how the illness arose, but what makes the visual jar model even more compelling is that you can use that same model to demonstrate the mechanism by which recovery occurs—by exerting control over environmental factors, and introducing protective factors (see Figure 4.7), such that symptoms are reduced or disappear. Examples of interventions to reduce risk may include psychiatric care, abstaining from illicit drugs, social support, and good self-care. You can explain how such interventions may be protective; that is, they partially "block" the opening of the jar so that it is more difficult to add to the overall risk.

"People who have never experienced an episode of psychiatric illness, but who are concerned about their risks because they have an affected family member, can also use protective factors."

Though they cannot change their level of genetic risk, individuals who have never experienced mental illness can make use of protective factor strategies such as those listed above to reduce their chances of developing symptoms (see Figure 4.8).

Issues That Clients and Their Families May Raise

"But no one else in my family has psychiatric illness—does this mean that I don't have any genetic vulnerability?"

This is a really common question to encounter from individuals who have no family history of mental illness. The jar model can be very helpful in addressing this issue. You can explain that the client's parents could easily have had genetic vulnerability to mental illness but never developed the illness, because their jars never became full—they never had the experiences that would have been necessary to fill the

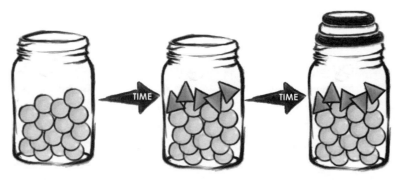

Figure 4.8. This picture shows that "protective factors" can be employed not only to aid recovery from an active episode of illness, but also to reduce the chance of the onset of a first episode for those individuals who might be more vulnerable. This kind of picture can be really useful to use if you are talking with parents of a child who has a higher chance for developing mental illness.

jar to the top. Remind the client that it seems that we all have some genetic vulnerability to mental illness, so even family members who were not affected would likely have had some genetic vulnerability. It could be that both of an affected individual's parents each only had a relatively small amount of genetic vulnerability in their jars, but the affected individual inherited all of the genetic vulnerability from both parents, resulting in significantly greater risk to develop mental illness (see Figure 4.9).

"How do I know how much genetic vulnerability is in my jar?"

This is something that many people want to know, and essentially, the answer is that at present we cannot know the answer for certain. There are clues that may give some idea about how much genetic vulnerability is in a person's jar, but this is not an exact science. For example, we expect that someone who has lots of affected family members over several generations is likely to have more genetic vul-

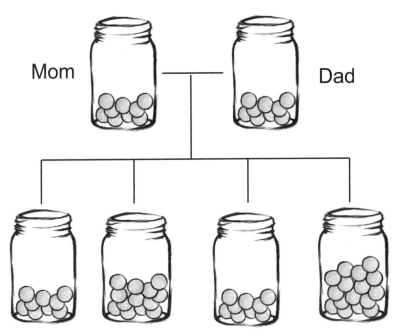

Figure 4.9. This picture shows, in modified pedigree format, how genetic vulnerability to mental illness may be transmitted within families. One of the key points to make explicit is that it is only the genetic vulnerability that is directly passed from generation to generation.

nerability factors in his or her jar than someone with no affected relatives at all. Similarly, we might imagine that someone who first experienced symptoms of mental illness at an unusually young age might have more genetic vulnerability in his or her jar (i.e., it took less time for the jar to fill up) than someone who was older when he or she experienced the first symptoms of mental illness. These are rough approximations, however, and we cannot, at present, definitively measure the degree to which an individual is genetically vulnerable to mental illness.

"I feel like I made some bad choices—for example, using drugs—that filled up my mental illness jar. Is it my fault that I developed psychiatric illness?"

This is a big fear that many people have, though they may not voice it. It is really important to find a way to determine the cause of and address guilt. In this case, the individual is potentially moving toward self-blame for the onset of his illness, which may increase his distress. It would be important to remind this person that usually no single factor causes mental illness; rather, mental illness usually arises due to a combination of factors.

It can be helpful to reflect that we make the decisions that we do in the context of our circumstances at the time, and that as circumstances change, so can our decisions. You can attempt to redirect the client toward a more empowering side of this concept: Because we can exert some control over our mental health, we can protect ourselves for the future.

"Did my upbringing cause me to develop psychiatric illness, or is it somehow my fault?"

Although the straightforward answer to this two-part question is strictly no, your upbringing alone did not cause your illness and it is not your fault, a preferable response would be, again, to reflect that it sounds like there is a real need for answers about what is to blame for the illness, and to offer to have a thorough discussion about the factors that are known to contribute to the development of psychiatric illness.

"How did environmental factor X play a role in causing my/my family member's psychiatric illness?"

In most cases we do not have an exact explanation for how a particular environmental factor increases risk for, or triggers the symptoms of a psychiatric illness. It is useful to help clients understand the idea of vulnerability or susceptibility; that is, affected individuals were born with some level of genetic risk, and different environmental exposures add to that baseline level of risk, moving a person closer and closer to illness onset.

"I have psychiatric illness because my mom had a psychiatric illness and she passed on her genetic vulnerability to me. So it seems like it's her fault that I have this illness, right?"

It is really important to note when an individual is searching for someone or something to blame for his or her illness and to address this issue forthrightly. Blame of self or other is often associated with increased distress. It is important to remind people that usually no single factor causes mental illness; rather, mental illness usually arises due to a combination of factors. It is also important to point out that it is not possible to control what genetic information we pass on and what we don't. Although most people would like to pass on only the best of their characteristics to their children, this is beyond human control—it comes down to chance.

"Can I give a psychiatric illness to my children?"

The most concise correct answer to this question would be this: "Children of people with psychiatric illnesses have higher chances of developing a psychiatric illness themselves than people whose parents do not have this illness, but the illness is generally not passed directly from parents to children." Using the jar analogy, you can explain that parents pass along the genetic risk that is in any person's jar, but it would be extremely rare for parents to pass along a full jar (indicating inevitable illness). We encourage you to use this opening to investigate whether this would be a good opportunity to find out more about the client's perception of cause of illness and risk to children, and discuss these issues in more detail.

"If I have children, do I pass on my environmental vulnerability factors, or just the genetic vulnerability factors?"

This possibility is a source of great concern, particularly to people who have personally experienced active episodes of mental illness. It can be useful to help clients understand that their children do not "inherit" the environmental risk factors experienced by them as a parent—that is, although the parents can pass along their genetic risk, most or all of the environmental risk factors accumulate over time. Some environmental risk factors tend to be shared in successive generations (e.g., poor dietary habits), though some research suggests that the most important environmental risk factors are those that are not shared by relatives (Tsuang, Stone, & Faraone, 2001). Considering this question on a deeper level, it is important to appreciate the genetic components to some of the proposed risk factors—for example, stressful life experiences or substance abuse. As we have discussed already, it is likely that genetic variants affect how people respond to stress and how much people seek out, and how they respond to, substance use. These genetic variants are passed through families, so while "stress," per se, may not be passed to children, parents may pass on a predisposition to respond poorly to stressful life events.

Our Experience

Often, in the beginning of discussions about causes of illness, people tend to assume anything related to genetics to be beyond their comprehension. In our experience, there is a pattern in how affected individuals and their families respond to these tools. Initially, there may be some hesitancy to engage with the material, perhaps based on the assumption that it will be too difficult to understand, but quickly, with the jar model and use of the individual's own family history, people sit forward in their seats, becoming more interested and engaged, and are keen to ask questions and share their perspective on how the information presented matches their own experience or intuition. They are also often keen to share their new knowledge with family members.

Case Example

Sarah was diagnosed with schizophrenia as a teenager, and one of her parents had the same diagnosis. Now in her early 30s, she had been successfully treated with an antipsychotic and had not experienced an acute illness episode for several years. She had a partner, was studying at a university, and felt settled and stable. Based on her own history and her family history (having an affected parent), she felt almost certain that any child she could have would have schizophrenia as well. She expressed to me (JA) that she wanted the illness to go no further in her family line than herself. In addition, her experience over years of interactions with health-care professionals who had overtly or covertly discouraged her from having a family of her own had led her to believe that she should not consider having children. Despite this, a quiet, small hope for a child led her to make sure she had her facts right, and she came for genetic counseling. When Sarah learned about the mechanisms by which schizophrenia arises, and that her potential child's mental health was not a foregone conclusion (although her child would have a higher chance of developing schizophrenia or some other kinds of mental illness than a child of someone who did not have schizophrenia and a family history of schizophrenia, there was also a large chance that the child would not be affected), she was elated. I discussed with Sarah the potential impact of pregnancy on her own mental health. We also discussed the difficulty of not having control over the illness risk or the ability to prevent a child from getting ill, and raising a child with the natural fears about whether he or she may be starting to exhibit symptoms. My goal as the counselor in this scenario was to ensure that Sarah's understanding of the illness causation was correct and to help her understand that mental illness was not a certainty for her potential child. It was also important that I temper her excitement at this news with realism—that her child would have a greater chance of developing mental illness than children of mothers who did not have schizophrenia. While this point was challenging, I aimed to help Sarah feel empowered to consider and discuss options for childbearing with her partner in light of complete and accurate information.

Case Example

Jill and Dan were recently married and were keen to start a family, but because Dan had been diagnosed with bipolar disorder, they were concerned about their children's chances of developing mental illness. They were interested in how experiences help determine whether an individual develops mental illness. Dan, in particular, was eager to find practical strategies by which to prevent their child from developing mental illness. The couple attended a presentation I (JA) had given, where I mentioned that children whose delivery was complicated (e.g., by anoxia) have been shown by some studies to have a higher chance of developing certain kinds of mental illness in later life. Dan asked whether, based on this information, I would suggest that they request a planned cesarean section for their child as a way to reduce the chance for delivery complications and thereby prevent mental illness later. I explained that none of the experiences I had talked about was either necessary or sufficient to cause mental illness, and so simply removing one potential risk factor could not prevent the potential for illness in later life. I also explained that there may be experiences that can contribute to the development of mental illness that have not yet been documented, and that perhaps by attempting to control for one (i.e., opting for a planned a c-section), it may be that the child is unwittingly exposed to another. In this situation my primary goal was to ensure that Dan and Jill both understood that there are no guarantees—no set formula for preventing mental illness. I also wanted to acknowledge that it was obvious that they both wanted the best for their children and would do everything in their power to give them the best chance for mental health, and that they would strive to be good parents. I wanted to ensure that they knew which actions they could take to protect against (but not prevent) mental health problems: the basic but undervalued triad of sleep, nutrition, and exercise, as well as having good social support networks and strategies for dealing with stress. I also described the importance of having open and honest conversations with teens about the different risks associated with having a family member with a mental illness that they may face, including the increased risk related to experimenting with street drugs such as cannabis or crystal meth. After discussing these points at length, we reflected together on how raising a child in the context of that uncertainty, without guarantees, would be hard. I reassured them that should "the worst" happen and their child develop symptoms, they would be better placed than most families, because they were familiar with the presentation of mental illness, to recognize the symptoms and get appropriate help quickly. I pointed out that getting the appropriate help as quickly as possible increasingly seems to be associated with good long-term prognosis. This perspective seemed to resonate with the couple. I felt that they left not with what they had wanted coming into the session—a recipe for absolute control over the prevention of mental illness—but with a more realistic appraisal of their situation, and some sense of empowerment.

Case Example

Maria was a single young adult whose mother and brother were affected with mood disorders. Maria, however, had not experienced any significant mood symptoms. She came for a consultation with me (HP) because she was very concerned about her own risk for a mood disorder. Besides asking questions about her level of risk, Maria was very interested in discussing how her lifestyle and exposures might affect her risk. Maria felt that her upbringing was quite turbulent, due to her mother's mood issues and her father's substance abuse. She perceived her upbringing as a very strong strike against her mental health. She cut all ties with her family as soon as she became independent because she felt that she could not maintain a good mental balance with the demands and negative energies surrounding her family. Since leaving home, Maria had made concerted efforts to surround herself with supportive, mentally stable friends to maintain a healthy lifestyle, and to keep close track of her own moods. Regardless of these efforts, she continued to be quite concerned, and on several occasions has sought therapy to help her cope with her fears about her mental health.

My goal for the session was to be listen fully to Maria's concerns and reflect back the anxiety related to her high level of fear, but also to reinforce the courageous and serious efforts that she had taken to protect her own mental health. We discussed the effects that uncertainty about her own mental health and her lack of ability to control the potential for illness onset has had on her happiness and life choices. We discussed how the uncertainty might change in coming years; Maria rightly felt that she would have less of a chance to develop a mood disorder as she grew older. We also discussed what it might mean to Maria if she were to develop symptoms. I encouraged her to maintain her relationship with a therapist for several reasons. First, Maria had significant issues related to her childhood and upbringing that would benefit from additional therapy. Second, the therapy could help her deal with her uncertainty about her own mental health. Finally, the therapist could partner with Maria to identify any early symptoms of a mood disorder, should symptoms occur.

Case Example

Alfred and Joan requested a consultation with me (HP) because they were planning to adopt a baby boy who was to be born in a few weeks. The couple had been overjoyed to find out that the infant was coming and had been preparing for his arrival. Their enthusiasm was converted to anxiety, however, when they found out that the birth mother was diagnosed with schizophrenia. They felt guilty to be second-guessing their interest in adopting the infant, but they were extremely concerned about knowingly accepting a child with a higher risk for the disorder. After some discussion, Alfred admitted that he had a great-uncle with the disorder who was severely affected and had not accepted treatment. Alfred found his great-uncle terrifying. Alfred stated that he would never be able to handle such a condition in his child, and Joan agreed. The couple asked whether taking the baby out of a "bad" home environment (that of the affected mother) and putting him into a "good" home environment (theirs) would allow them to control the risk. I reviewed the research that suggests that home environment is unlikely to cause or prevent psychiatric illness—with the caveat, however, that we do not know in any individual exactly what may prevent illness. I discussed the importance of a supportive, stable home environment for any child. I described the known or suspected environmental risk factors in relation to the baby's prenatal history and what might come in the future. The birth mother had received good prenatal care and had been mentally stable during her pregnancy, and the birth father was healthy and young—factors that potentially reduced some risk. We discussed how Alfred and Joan might be especially careful about messages related to substance use when the baby was a young teenager, if they chose to adopt him. I quantified the risk for schizophrenia in the baby, but I also reminded the couple that no baby is at no risk for mental illness. Finally, I reminded the couple that our knowledge about the causes of schizophrenia and our ability to effectively treat the condition may be considerably more advanced by the time the baby reached early adulthood. I spent several sessions facilitating the couple's decision making and helping them appreciate the potential emotional ramifications of either choice.

Case Example

Tracy, now in her late 30s, was diagnosed with schizoaffective disorder in her early 20s. Tracy had just learned that one of her teenage cousins had recently been diagnosed with bipolar disorder, and this had prompted her to want to gather as much information as she could to finally understand the cause of her illness. Because the cause of her illness had been a nagging question for years, she took her cousin's diagnosis as an impetus to seek out genetic counseling. During documentation of her family history, Tracy told me (JA) that in addition to her own diagnosis and that of her cousin, she was aware that her aunt had been diagnosed with some kind of mental illness, but that she didn't know what the diagnosis was, because in her family discussing the topic was taboo. However, she did know that the aunt had displayed many symptoms that Tracy now recognized as similar to her own, and indeed had been hospitalized on multiple occasions as Tracy was growing up. When I asked Tracy to tell me what she thought caused her illness, she replied that she had heard it was caused by a "chemical imbalance in the brain," but she couldn't work out how the brain chemicals would get imbalanced in the first place. She also told me that when reflecting on her aunt's illness, and that of her cousin, she had also started wondering whether her illness was somehow genetic, but she was confused about how—if that were the case—she and her cousin could have different diagnoses. However, Tracy was also quite certain that events that preceded her first psychotic break somehow triggered her illness. Each of the things she told me that she had considered as potential explanations for illness seemed to her to be quite disparate, with a net result being that she felt very uncertain about the cause of her illness and tended to vacillate between different explanations depending on her circumstance—an experience she found to be very unsatisfying. In the course of the next hour, by using the jar model and her own unique family history, I was able to show Tracy that her thoughts about the cause of her illness were, in fact, correct, and I was able to help her tie all of the pieces together into one coherent story that included the elements of genetics and environment, and how both relate to chemical imbalance in the brain. She understood how different biological relatives can have different mental illness diagnoses based on there being a shared underlying genetic vulnerability to mental illness in general. Tracy was visibly delighted with her new understanding and let me know a few weeks later that she had shared her new knowledge with her cousin.

Case Example

David had a diagnosis of bipolar disorder. Now in his mid-40s, he had been living with his condition for two decades. He came for genetic counseling essentially because he was bewildered at the stories he had heard about bipolar disorder being "genetic." He told me (JA) that he was sure that the people who had told him this were well informed, but the story just didn't make sense to him. This was not only because he was the only person in his sizable family with mental illness of any kind, but also because he was certain that a series of very stressful life events that immediately preceded his first manic episode were directly responsible for causing his illness. I explained to David how twin and adoption studies showed that genetics seems to be important in contributing to the development of bipolar disorder, but that experiences are also important in determining whether we develop mental illness. I used the jar model to show David how these factors might have contributed to his particular illness, and how it is, in fact, very common to find that an individual with a mental illness such as bipolar disorder has no affected family members at all, despite the importance of genetics. David engaged enthusiastically in the discussion, telling me that he felt validated that he was likely right in thinking that his stressful life events contributed to his manic episode, and was also satisfied to understand how genetics could be relevant to him, despite the fact that he had no affected relatives.

CHAPTER FIVE

Evaluating and Assessing Risk

The information collected when taking a family history (described in Chapter 3) allows you to personalize the risk evaluation. The process of personalizing a risk assessment allows for an explanation of risk (as described in Chapter 6) that is more accurate and meaningful for clients. This chapter includes information on how to think through a basic risk assessment; a discussion of the origin, benefits, and limitations of the recurrence risks established by empirical research; a review of factors that confound the application of empiric recurrence risks; and details about individual and family characteristics that indicate increased or reduced family risk. We also provide examples of family risk evaluation.

Risk assessment is unique for each presenting client and family. It can be performed with different degrees of depth and rigor. The ability to provide in-depth risk assessment is a skill that requires a strong genetics knowledge base, familiarity with the research literature, and a lot of practice. This type of risk assessment is often best left to genetics professionals or to mental health professionals who specialize in genetics. However, a basic risk evaluation, with a primary goal of evaluating whether the "empiric risks" derived from research data are reasonably appropriate for a particular family, is relatively simple to provide and is of great use to many clients. We encourage you to use the tips and tools in this chapter to provide a basic risk evaluation for clients and families.

Keep in mind that discussions about risk for psychiatric illness should include a focus on the causes of the psychiatric illness, because without a basic understanding of the causes, clients will have no context within which to understand how risk is evaluated. For details on how to discuss the factors that contribute to the development of psychiatric illness with clients and families, please see Chapter 4.

What Does Research Tell Us about Risk?

Empirically, risk is increased. Research studies have provided reasonably well-established estimates of risk for close relatives of individuals affected by schizophrenia (Austin & Peay, 2006), bipolar disorder (Smoller & Finn, 2003), major depression (Maier et al., 1992), autism (Bolton et al., 1994), OCD (Rasmussen & Tsuang, 1986), and other psychiatric illnesses. These estimates of risk are generated by considering the frequency with which a given psychiatric illness occurs within a large cohort of individuals who share a common kind of relationship to an affected individual (e.g., siblings). The risk estimates generated from such studies are termed "empiric recurrence risks." As might be expected, these recurrence risk estimates vary between studies. Despite this variation, as shown in Table 5.1, there is fairly good consistency across studies that evaluate empiric risks; discrepancies may largely be attributable to the use of different diagnostic criteria and methods of ascertainment between studies, differing ages at assessment of subjects, and true variation in observed rate of illness. Because of these discrepancies, we recommend that you use a risk *range* rather than a single risk *number* based on one study. Tables 5.1 and 5.2 list the risks of schizophrenia and bipolar disorder respectively in relatives of affected individuals.

Table 5.1. Empirically Derived, Lifetime Risks (%) for Schizophrenia among Relatives of Affected Individuals, from Selected Publications

Relationship to individual with schizophrenia	Parent	Child (1 affected parent)	Child (2 affected parents)	Sibling	Sibling (1 affected parent)	MZ Twin	DZ Twin	Grand-child	Half-Sib	Niece Nephew	Uncle Aunt	Cousin
					Morbid risks (%) for schizophrenia based on relationship of individual to affected relative(s)							
Gottesman, 1991* [7]	6	13	46	9	17	48	17	5	6	4	2	2
Vogel & Motulsky, 1997# [8]	5.6	12.8	—	9.6	16.7	—	—	3.7	4.2	—	3	2.4
Harper. 1998 [3]^	—	13	45	9	15	40	10	3	3	3	3	1-2
Papadimitriou, 2003 [6]^	—	13	50	10	17	50	—	5	5	5	5	1-2

Study											
Sham et al., 1994 [4]	7.4**	7.4**	—	7.4**	—	—	—	—	—	—	—
Waddington & Youssef, 1996 [2]	1.4	—	—	8.3	—	—	—	—	—	—	—
Kendler et al., 1993 [9]	1.3	—	—	9.2	—	—	—	—	—	—	—
Parnas et al., 1993 [5]	—	16.2	—	—	—	—	—	—	—	—	—
Niemi et al., 2004 [10]	—	6.7	—	—	—	—	—	—	—	—	—

*Data compiled from all (n = 40) systematic twin and family studies in European samples between 1920 and 1987.

#Each risk figure represents data compiled from between 3 and 14 studies, and may not be independent to other figures.

**Compiled results for all first-degree relatives.

^Sources of data not quoted.

ADAPTED FROM AUSTIN AND PEAY (*Clinical Genetics*, 2006).

Table 5.2. Lifetime Risks for Bipolar Disorder (Gottesman et al., 2010; Smoller & Finn, 2003)

Relationship to individual with BD	Lifetime risk (%)
Parent	5–10%
Sibling	5–20%
Child (2 affected parents)	25%
Child (1 affected parent)	5–10%
MZ twin	45–70%
DZ twin	5–20%

A Note about How Recurrence Risks Can Be Expressed

Information about the risk of a disorder occurring in a family member of an affected individual can be expressed in a number of different ways. For example:

- *Lifetime absolute risk:* "Siblings of individuals with schizophrenia have a X% (or X in 100) chance of also developing schizophrenia."
- *Relative risk:* "Siblings of individuals with schizophrenia are X times more likely than a person in the general population to develop schizophrenia."

It is important to know which statistic is being reported: absolute or relative. For schizophrenia and bipolar I disorder, for each of which the lifetime population prevalence is approximately 1%, there is little difference between the absolute and relative risks—that is, a sibling may have a 10% chance to develop schizophrenia *or* be 10 times more likely than someone in the general population to develop schizophrenia. But, for other disorders (e.g., autism or depression) for which population prevalences are considerably different from 1%, there can be a very large difference between lifetime and relative risks.

Risk Moves Through Generations

If you recall basic genetic principles (see Chapter 1), you will remember that a parent passes to a child one of his or her two alleles for each gene. Thus with each child, a parent has a 50% chance of passing along a particular version of each gene—perhaps the allele that increases risk, or perhaps the allele that does not increase risk. This "shuffling" of alleles in each child helps to ensure variation in our species, and also means that there is a wide range of risk that can be passed from parents to children. Keep in mind that additional genetic susceptibility might be added at each mating from the other parent.

Risk Is Increased for More Than One Disorder

So far in this chapter, we have discussed the risks for relatives of an individual with a particular psychiatric illness to develop *the same* psychiatric illness themselves. However, for first-degree relatives of individuals with most psychiatric illnesses, including schizophrenia, bipolar disorder, major depression, anxiety disorders, and pervasive developmental disorders, we know that in addition to having higher risks than the general population to develop the same condition as the affected family member, there are additional risks to develop etiologically related spectrum disorders. For example, a first-degree relative of someone with schizophrenia would have additional risks of developing a schizophrenia spectrum disorder (which include schizoaffective disorder, schizotypal personality disorder, and paranoid personality disorder) (Laursen et al., 2005). In addition, for relatives of individuals with both schizophrenia and bipolar disorder, risks for unipolar (major) depression are also increased (Kendler & Gardner, 1997).

There Are Gaps in Available Empiric Risk Data

Despite the fact that these empiric recurrence risks are reasonably well established, they are available for only a relatively limited range of relationships—siblings, children, parents, or cousins of affected individuals. In addition, in most cases, there are no empiric recurrence risks that take into account the following factors:

- Occurrence of multiple distinct psychiatric diagnoses in a single family
- Individuals with uncertain diagnoses or symptomatic, undiagnosed individuals, multiple individuals with the same diagnosis within multiple generations (empiric recurrence risks are not available for more than a handful of combinations of two or more affected family members, as shown in Table 5.1)
- Affected individuals on both sides of the family, except in cases where both parents are affected.

You will find that the practical application of empiric recurrence risks is often confounded because one or more of the factors listed above is commonly found in a given family. Indeed, you will find that empiric recurrence risk data exactly reflect the presenting family structure only infrequently.

How Should I Evaluate the "Fit" of Empiric Risk Data?

Even in the rare cases when a client's family history exactly matches a family structure for which empiric risk data are available, keep in mind the limitations that apply to empirically established risks: *These risks are averaged from a research population. They are neither constant over a lifetime nor without variation between individuals.* Factors that influence an individual's risk for psychiatric illness and thus allow you to evaluate the fit of empiric risk data include the following.

Characteristics of the Affected Family Member(s)
- *Consider the age at onset of illness symptoms.* A young age at time of onset could indicate greater genetic vulnerability, and an in-

creased genetic vulnerability in the affected individual could mean that his or her relatives may have more genetic vulnerability and higher risk for illness.

- *Evaluate illness severity.* Would the illness be classified as on the more severe end of the spectrum, compared to others with that diagnosis? This too might indicate greater genetic vulnerability. For example, relatives of individuals with type 1 bipolar disorder with psychosis seem to have higher risks of developing illness themselves than relatives of individuals with type 1 bipolar disorder without psychosis (Smoller & Finn, 2003).

Characteristics of the Individual for Whom You Are Estimating Risk

- *Consider the age of the at-risk individual compared to the typical age at disorder onset.* For example, the typical age at onset for schizophrenia is during the late teens or early 20s. Risk for developing schizophrenia is lower in the first decade of life, increases through the second, and decreases through the third and subsequent decades. Initial onset of schizophrenia after the age of 50, regardless of whether someone has an affected family member, would be very uncommon.
- *Take into account mental health history*, where existing symptoms would suggest that an at-risk person is more likely to develop a psychiatric disorder. For example, if you have been asked to provide information about the risk of bipolar disorder for someone who has a parent with the condition, and you discover that this individual has recently been diagnosed with ADHD, or has already had several episodes of depression, his or her risk for developing bipolar disorder may be higher (Spencer et al., 2001).
- *Consider the sex of the individual for whom you are calculating risk.* As you are aware, there are disorders that have skewed male-to-female ratios, such as major depression and autism, and individuals of the more-often affected sex are empirically at higher risk. There is some evidence about sex effects in other disorders, but the data are not consistent and the associated risk seems to be relatively low.

Characteristics of the Family

- *Consider the family structure.* Does the individual for whom you are calculating risk have only one affected family member or multiple affected family members? A greater number of affected family members usually indicates greater genetic vulnerability and therefore greater risk to family members of affected individuals.
- *Consider both sides of the family.* In situations where both sides of the family are affected, it is impossible to determine if the risk factors on one side are the same as risk factors on the other side, and because the vulnerabilities conferred by each side may be different, it is not clear what the cumulative effect would be. It is reasonable to assume, however, that risk is increased if the at-risk individual inherits susceptibility from both sides of the family.

Application Example

The following scenario presents an example of an oversimplified and incorrect application of empiric risks, followed by a more correct application.

A client with schizophrenia has a sister who is concerned about her risk of also developing schizophrenia. You find that the empiric risk for a sibling of someone with schizophrenia to develop the same condition is about 8–15%. You tell the sister, "Your risk of developing schizophrenia is about 8–15%."

Why is this answer incorrect? Remember that empiric risks are population-based risks. Risk for psychiatric illness varies over the lifetime and between individuals, so empiric risks cannot accurately be applied like this to any particular individual.

Why is this answer oversimplified? Essentially, without knowing more about the sister (e.g., her age, current mental status, and family history), we cannot know whether the empiric risk data are a good fit for her particular situation.

To illustrate: If the sister is 50 years old when you speak with her and has had no mental health problems at all in the past, it is very unlikely indeed that she would now develop schizophrenia. Her risk of developing schizophrenia would be considerably less than even the lowest end of the risk range (8%), so in this case the empiric risks do not fit the family situation very well. *Given these additional details, the empiric risk is an overestimate.*

If the sister is 15 years old and has recently been experiencing non-specific lowered mood, anxiety, and social withdrawal, she is likely at considerably greater risk than even the higher end of the risk range (15%) for developing schizophrenia—indeed, it could be that she is currently experiencing prodromal symptoms (Yung et al., 2003). *Given these additional details, the empiric risk is an underestimate.*

If the sister is 15 years old and, in addition to the single affected sister that we know about in the original scenario, another of her three older siblings is also affected, as is one of her parents, her risk would again be substantially higher than even the higher end of the risk range (15%) that was quoted as being her risk. *Given these additional details, the empiric risk is an underestimate.*

Empiric recurrence risks should be used as a foundation for estimating the risk that the disorder may happen again in a particular family, but in order to use the data appropriately, it is important to individualize them as much as possible. In the example above, a better response to the scenario might be the following:

"If we look at the empiric risks for schizophrenia for someone who has an affected sibling, we can see that, in general, 8–15% of siblings of an individual with schizophrenia will develop that condition themselves. But we know that if someone is going to develop schizophrenia, the symptoms usually begin during the late teens or early 20s. You are 50 years old, so we could estimate that your risk to develop schizophrenia is probably a lot lower than even the lower end of that risk range (8%)."

Tips for Incorporating Risk Assessment into Practice

We appreciate that risk assessment is complex and may seem overwhelming to many clinicians. Take the process one step at a time. At minimum, consider the following, which we consider to be the most important "red flags" for increased risk:

- Many affected relatives. Especially look for:
  - ° Multiple affected individuals over several generations, especially when the affected relatives are closely related to each other and to the at-risk individual
  - ° Several affected siblings in one family, when the at-risk individual is one of the siblings or a child of one of the siblings
  - ° Close relatives on both sides of the family who are affected, especially when one or both parents of the at-risk individual is affected.
- Early ages at symptom onset for disorders that typically have adult onset. Especially look for childhood or adolescent onset.
- Symptoms in the "unaffected" at-risk person, which may be early prodromal symptoms.
- Young age of the at-risk person, indicating that he or she still has most of his or her lifetime risk ahead.

The most important flag of *decreased risk* is an at-risk relative who has lived through a good portion of his or her risk—for example, an unaffected individual in her late 40s in a family with bipolar disorder.

Again, taking a stepwise approach, it may be useful to consider the following items as you think through how to individualize empiric risks.

- *Determine who in the family is affected, and with which disorders.* Consider the number of affected individuals and their characteristics, including age at onset, severity of symptoms, and sex.
- *Determine who is at risk, for which disorders.* Include characteristics of the at-risk person, including age, sex, and current and past mental status.
- *Put parameters around risk assessment.* When evaluating the family history to determine the best estimate of risk for illness, it can be

helpful for you to keep in mind the constraints of what may be the upper and lower limits of risk for psychiatric illness. Until we know enough to attribute protective genetic and environmental factors to risk, the lower limit of the risk will always be the population risk for that disorder; for example, approximately 1% for either schizophrenia or bipolar disorder and 10–20% for major depression. The true upper limit of the risk for psychiatric illness is unknown, but for all but the very highest-risk situations, 50% is likely to be a reasonable estimation of an upper limit. It is important to note that in most cases, however, an upper limit of 50% will grossly overestimate risk. The 50% figure roughly approximates the risk for (1) an identical twin of an individual with psychiatric illness (Cardno et al., 1999); (2) an individual who has two parents affected with the same psychiatric illness (Gottesman et al., 2010); (3) an individual who has multiple affected family members in multiple generations; and (4) a young person who has an affected first-degree relative and who has recently started experiencing nonspecific lowered mood and social withdrawal (Yung et al., 2003).

• *Ask the key question: "Given what I know about this individual's personal and family history, how well do I think that the empiric risks estimate the actual magnitude of risk in this case?"* In many cases, our knowledge is not adequate to allow for an accurate *quantitative* modification of risk for any individual client, but research provides us with ample data with which to *qualitatively* modify risk to better match individual history. Think of empiric risks as indicating an approximate magnitude of risk, *if* the client's data are a reasonable match to the medical and family history. If you are less experienced with risk assessment and less knowledgeable about the research literature, you may feel most comfortable explaining to clients whether their risk is likely to be less than the empiric risk, similar in magnitude, or more than the empiric risk. More experienced clinicians may wish to go a step further and use the research data and their clinical experience to focus and narrow the upper and lower risk limits that they use in the risk assessment (e.g., modify the more general estimate of a lower limit of 1% and an upper limit of 50% to a more specific estimate of a lower limit of 30% and upper limit of 50%, based on the client and family history). A detailed discussion of how to do this is beyond the scope of this book, but referral to a genetics specialist for this type of risk evaluation is appropriate. See the section called "How and when to make a referral to a genetics specialist" later in this chapter (on page 127), and the Appendix for resources regarding making referrals to genetics.

Once you have thought through risk assessment in a stepwise fashion, explain to the client and family why the empiric risk data fit their particular family situation, or why the data do not. In other words, explain why you think their specific risk in question is higher or lower than the empiric risks might suggest. We find that it is useful to walk clients and family members through our thinking in a very similar manner to what was described above. For example:

"These are the people who are affected. . . ."
"These are the people who seem to have the most risk. . . ."
"These are the disorders I'm most concerned about in terms of risk. . . ."
"I noticed the following indicators of increased risk in your family history. . . ."
"This is the empirical risk range based on the literature. . . . "
"Here is how well I think the range estimates your family risk."

Spotting "Red Flags" for Genetic Syndromes That Include Psychiatric Features

Just when you thought you might be catching on to family risk assessment . . . let's get back to the genetic syndromes that we mentioned in Chapter 1. It is important to remember that even taken together, these syndromes are rare, accounting for probably only a few percent of those affected with major psychiatric illnesses of adult onset. Because they are so rare, it is not important that you memorize the disorders or their features, but rather simply be aware of the red flags that suggest increased likelihood of a genetic syndrome. If the family or medical history raises suspicions of a genetic syndrome because one or more of these red flags is present, we recommend a referral to a genetics specialist for a consultation and exam. In situations where the psychiatric illness occurs in the context of a genetic syndrome, family risks will often be very different from empirical risk estimates that we have been discussing in this chapter. Red flags indicating increased likelihood of the presence of a genetic syndrome include:

- A history of birth defects (e.g., cleft lip, cardiac abnormalities, clubbed foot), especially in individuals who also have psychiatric symptoms
- A history of learning problems or intellectual disability, especially in individuals who also have psychiatric symptoms
- A history of unusual health problems, especially in individuals who also have psychiatric symptoms
- A multigenerational family history of psychiatric illness, especially when combined with any of the red flags listed above.

In addition to the fact that for many of the syndromes, the risk for additional family members to be affected may be quite different than for psychiatric illness that is unrelated to a genetic syndrome, it is important to identify families with genetic syndromes because there may be additional health risks and different treatment recommendations. In addition, much more accurate genetic risk assessment and in some cases genetic testing are available for the syndromes.

Risk Assessment When the Client Has Autism

The syndrome red flags are important for all psychiatric disorders, but be especially cognizant of the importance of single-gene disorders and changes to chromosomes as causes of autism and other pervasive developmental disorders. An underlying genetic cause can currently be found in about 15% of cases of autism seen in clinical genetics clinics (Schaefer et al., 2008), and that number is expected to rise with the advent of new genetic testing capabilities. All clients with autism benefit from an evaluation by a genetics professional to determine whether genetic testing is appropriate and which tests might be most informative.

Challenges to Incorporating Risk Assessment into Practice

The major challenges in the risk assessment process include deciding who to count as affected, taking into account the spectrum of illness and the illness age at onset, and the occurrence of psychiatric illness on both sides of the family. These challenges are further described in the text that follows.

Determining Who Is Affected

As we have described, risk assessment depends on evaluating the pattern of both affected and unaffected individuals in the family. However, establishing whether someone is affected or unaffected is not always straightforward, for the reasons described below.

- *More than one diagnosis in the family.* For example, let's say you are evaluating a family history to provide a basic risk assessment for an individual who has an affected parent to develop bipolar disorder. You notice that in addition to the affected parent, there are other close biological relatives who have had diagnoses of major depression, ADHD, and schizoaffective disorder. Should these relatives be counted as "affected" or "unaffected" for the purposes of risk assessment in this situation? It is important to remember that the factors that can increase vulnerability to bipolar disorder are not thought to be specific to bipolar disorder. Rather, it seems that these factors can increase vulnerability to psychiatric illness more broadly, and that the particular combination of vulnerability factors found in a given individual determines what disorder he or she may eventually manifest. The particular group of disorders clustering in this family is likely to be closely related etiologically, implying shared factors that can increase risk for all of these illnesses in this family. Thus, it may be prudent to explain this to the individual for whom you are calculating risk, and err on the side of providing a "worst-case scenario risk estimate" by counting all of these relatives as affected. For a history as complex as that described above, a referral to a genetics professional is often appropriate.

- *Undiagnosed relatives.* A similar situation arises when a family history reveals members who did not have psychiatric diagnoses but who had, for example, "nervous breakdowns" or who are described as being "strange" or "loners." Gathering as much information as possible about such family members can be helpful in deciding whether to consider them as affected or unaffected for the purposes of risk assessment.

- *Substance misuse.* Family members who have issues with substance misuse raise other challenges. Alcoholism is a psychiatric diagnosis in its own right, but also reliance on substances may be a form of self-medication for other concurrent psychiatric conditions, so again determining whether to consider these individuals as affected or unaffected can be difficult. Whether or not you decide to include someone with substance misuse as affected, it is important that clients and families understand that risk for substance use may also be increased in the family.

Psychiatric illnesses that tend to have adolescent or adult onset add an additional element to the risk assessment because of the challenge of determining whether "unaffected" relatives are truly unaffected, or whether they will develop (or, if they have passed away, would have developed) psychiatric illness. Even if they were not affected, they may have had generic vulnerability that could be passed to subsequent generations, but it is impossible to know how much.

Unaffected individuals in a family with a psychiatric illness will be unaffected for one of the reasons below:

1. They have enough genetic and environmental risk to "fill the jar" (with "filling the jar" equating to illness onset; see Chapter 4 for a full explanation of the "jar model" of susceptibility) and will go on to develop illness in time, unless they die from another cause before expressing symptoms.
2. They have significant genetic risk, but insufficient environmental risk to "fill the jar" and/or protective environmental factors that reduce risk.
3. They have a small/moderate amount of genetic risk, and it is very unlikely that they will ever accumulate enough environmental vulnerability factors to "fill the jar."
4. They have very little genetic risk and thus it is very unlikely that they will acquire sufficient environmental exposures to "fill the jar" and cause illness.

At-risk individuals described under items 1 and 2 have a full complement of genetic risk that they may pass on to the next generation; recall the random 50% chance of passing each allele to a child. The at-risk individuals described under item 3 have a smaller amount of genetic risk that can be passed along to future generations, and those individuals may manifest illness if they accumulate sufficient additional vulnerability. The at-risk individuals described under item 4 will pass along little to no genetic risk to future generations.

Risk on Both Sides of the Family
It is not uncommon to find affected individuals on both sides of a family as a result of stochastic factors, the frequency of the disorder, and because of assortative mating (the tendency of individuals with psychiatric illness, or family histories of psychiatric illness, to choose each other as mates). At this time, it is not generally possible to determine how to integrate risk from both sides of the family. Empiric risk data that pertains to risk from both sides of the family are, at best, limited to a child who has two affected parents (Gottesman et al., 2010). We do not have sufficient data to support simply adding the empiric risks from both

sides of the family. The combined risk may be additive, but it also could be multiplicative, or some of the risk could cancel out.

How and When to Make a Referral to a Genetics Specialist

In deciding how and when to make a referral to a genetics specialist, you first must identify clients who might benefit from the referral. Some examples of clients who might benefit from such a referral include:

- Those who have personal or family histories that include one or more "red flags" described above.
- Those who request additional information or support around decision making or life planning related to genetic risk.
- Pregnant clients who are taking psychiatric medications.
- All clients with autism (these individuals should be evaluated by a pediatric geneticist to rule out genetic syndromes).

If in doubt about the need for referral or in the case of questions, it is appropriate to consult with the specialist before the referral.

Many major medical centers have a genetics center where clients can access genetic counseling. If a referral is necessary, locate the closest specialist or genetics center. Some genetics professionals have a special interest in psychiatric genetics; if someone who specializes in psychiatric genetics is available in your area, this is an added advantage. The majority of experienced genetics professionals have the training and knowledge necessary to provide a comprehensive consultation to your client. Note that some centers provide outreach clinics or telemedicine appointments for those in more rural areas or in smaller centers. A list of genetic counselors (searchable by name, area of interest, city, state, and medical center) is available at *www.nsgc .org*. A similar list that includes M.D. geneticists is available at *www .ashg.org*.

You should inform your clients of the purpose and potential benefits of genetic counseling, and you can help them identify medical and family information that will be necessary for risk assessment. It is helpful to inform a client that obtaining as much information as possible about his or her family history before the consultation will allow the genetic counselor to generate an estimate of risk that is as personalized as possible. With your client's permission, provide the genetic counselor with a brief overview of the client's psychiatric history and current diagnosis before the consultation with your client.

The genetic counselor will provide you with a summary of the consultation, which could be a fruitful area for further discussion with clients. You can further engage clients around risk-reduction efforts and support them in their decision-making efforts and life planning.

We strongly believe that the most effective way to serve clients is through partnerships between genetics professionals and mental health professionals. Unfortunately, for a long time psychiatric genetic counseling has been an area that many clinicians—including both those in clinical genetics and mental health—avoided. Happily, this is now changing, as genetics professionals increasingly provide information about more common, complex disorders (as opposed to single-gene conditions), and as mental health clinicians realize the important role of genetics in their clients' care. We are still a long way, however, from having informed clinicians available to the majority of clients. We believe that clients have much to gain from the development of closer, collaborative relationships between mental health clinicians and genetics professionals. In the same way that we encourage our genetics colleagues to build relationships with mental health clinicians, we invite mental health care clinicians to consider developing lasting relationships with genetics colleagues.

What You Can Say to Clients and Family Members about Risk Assessment

"Your family history and your own psychiatric history are vital to the risk assessment process."

Explaining that these are vital pieces of information is a good way to begin to talk about risks with clients and family members. It can also be helpful to explain that certain aspects of personal and family psychiatric history can influence risk for other family members to be affected. If you have already discussed the factors that contribute to the development of psychiatric illness (which is advisable before discussing risks), you can explain that by looking at personal and family psychiatric history you can begin to get an impression of how much genetic vulnerability is in the family (or "in the jar"), which in turn helps estimate risks.

"What psychiatric disorder(s) are you concerned about?"

It can be helpful to establish whether an individual is concerned about risks for a specific disorder, or for psychiatric illness in general. The answer to this question allows you to focus your efforts appropriately. It is important, though, to educate clients about the concept of the spectrum—that is, that there is risk for more than one disorder. Many clients may not be aware of this, and they will not be able to determine whether they want to receive risk information for psychiatric illness in general until they appreciate the risk for a wider set of disorders.

"It's important to remember that almost everyone has some risk for psychiatric illness, even people with no family history."

It is good to remind concerned family members or clients that psychiatric disorders are very common and that, empirically, everyone is at some level of risk. We find it useful to bring up this point at the beginning of a risk discussion, and to reiterate it as needed.

"Coming up with an estimate of risk for psychiatric illness is not an exact science, but by using these empiric risk numbers

together with information about you and your family, I can
give you an estimate of what your risk might be."

Explicitly acknowledging the limitations of the risk estimation process allows clients and family members to form more accurate expectations.

Issues That Clients and Their Families May Raise

"Where did these risk numbers come from?"

You can explain to the client that the numbers originate from research studies that generated empiric risks (see a potential explanation for empiric risks in above section), being very upfront about the benefits and limitations of the data. You could discuss (or review again) how the client's medical and family histories affect the application of empiric risks to his or her situation. Note that such a question might warrant your checking in to evaluate the motivation for the query. It may be that the number you provided was quite different from what the individual was expecting, and the client is finding it difficult to believe it.

"Why do you need to know about how old my relative was when
he [or she] got ill in order to give me an idea of what my risk is
to develop psychiatric illness?"

There are different motivations for this question and therefore different possible options for response. One possibility is that the client is curious and eager to evaluate his or her own family history. You could explain that one of the indicators for increased risks for family members is an early age at illness onset in the affected relative. The question also could indicate that this individual is finding it difficult, emotionally or practically, to answer your questions. You could reassure your client that it is normal not to be able to answer all of the questions asked during the family history, and suggest that even if he or she does not know the exact answer to the questions, any information can help you personalize the risk estimate as much as possible. You could also remind your client that others in the family may have more information about the family history and encourage him or her to obtain more information when possible, to add to the family history at a later visit.

Our Experience

Case Example

In this case, we are providing a risk estimation for the young man (age 15) indicated by the arrow on the pedigree in Figure 5.1. We took a

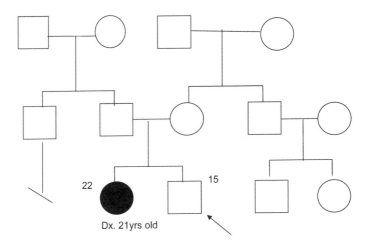

 Schizophrenia

Figure 5.1. The pedigree can be very helpful in allowing you to generate an estimate of the risk for a family member to develop mental illness. In this format, all of the information relevant to risk is clearly laid out. In this family, we are calculating risk for the young man indicated by the arrow. There are no markers indicating that risk would deviate from estimates from empiric risk figures.

detailed, targeted psychiatric family history. There is good information about the psychiatric history of all the family members in the pedigree, and his only affected family member is his older sister, who has a diagnosis of schizophrenia that was made last year, when she was 21 years old (which is a fairly typical age for illness onset). She experienced her first symptoms only months before her diagnosis. The young man himself reports no psychiatric problems, and his family reports no concerns about his mental health—he has friends, is active, does well at school, and is engaged with his family. In this situation, the empiric risk for a sibling of an individual affected with schizophrenia is the best possible fit for this young man with this particular family history, because there are no red flags indicating increased risk or markers for decreased risk.

Case Example

In this case we are again providing risk estimation for the young man (age 15) indicated by the arrow on the pedigree in Figure 5.2. As in the

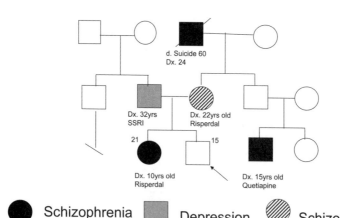

Figure 5.2. In this case, we are again using a pedigree. The risk we are calculating is again for the young man, but this time we can see that there are a number of "red flags" indicating that the risk for him to develop mental illness is likely higher than would be indicated by empiric risk figures.

previous case, we took a detailed targeted psychiatric family history. There is good information about the psychiatric history of all the family members in the pedigree, and the only affected family members are those identified. He has a sister who was diagnosed with schizophrenia when she was 10 years old, but in retrospect the family thinks that she had probably been sick (responding to command hallucinations) for 2 years prior to the diagnosis. The father of the young man has a history of recurrent depression, for which he takes a selective serotonin reuptake inhibitor (SSRI). The mother of the young man was diagnosed in her 20s with schizoaffective disorder. Like her daughter, she has been stable for many years on Risperdal. The maternal grandfather of the young man was diagnosed with schizophrenia; he committed suicide at age 60. A male maternal cousin of the young man was also recently diagnosed with schizophrenia and has just started taking quetiapine. The young man himself is quiet and withdrawn and answers questions posed to him with one or two words while looking at the floor. His parents are frustrated and concerned about him. They just found out that his grades have deteriorated at school, and that in the last week he has been skipping school. For this particular family history, the empiric risk for this young man to develop schizophrenia is probably a very poor fit, because there are many red flags indicating increased risk: (1) his sister was diagnosed at a very early age; (2) in addition to his affected sister, both of his parents have histories of psychiatric illness, as does a grandfather and a cousin; and (3) his behavior indicates that his own mental health might have started to deteriorate. It seems likely that his risk of developing psychiatric illness is considerably higher than would be indicated by the empirical risk. In this circumstance, a mental health evaluation for the young man in question is appropriate, and if the family members remain interested in discussing risks, referral to a genetic counselor might be appropriate as well (see section earlier in this chapter about how to make a referral to a genetics specialist).

CHAPTER SIX
_____

Explaining Risk

In the last chapter, we discussed how you might evaluate the level of risk in the family in relation to empiric risks, and derive an individualized risk estimate based on characteristics of the family. In this chapter, we focus on how to talk about this risk with your client and their family. The overall goal of family risk counseling is to personalize and effectively convey messages about risk for other family members to be affected.

Some mental health clinicians have told us that they are concerned that having discussions about family risk might be overly worrisome for clients and might adversely affect their therapeutic relationship. Certainly, you should take into account each client's status and the timing of the interaction; there will be clients for whom illness symptoms or other more pressing concerns make a discussion of family risk ill-advised. In addition, there will be a subset of clients for whom family risk counseling is simply not of interest or not warranted. The appropriateness of discussions about family risk should be considered on a case-by-case basis. Nevertheless, we encourage you to consider the benefits of information about risk that our experience leads us to believe are likely applicable to most of your clients.

Our clinical and research experience suggests that many clients and family members are *already* thinking about the potential for family risk, and would very much appreciate your willingness to discuss their concerns, evaluate and communicate their risk, and provide counsel about risk perception and life planning (Peay et al., 2009). Clients who are considering having children or already have children may use the information to make more informed reproductive decisions, appreciate the likely magnitude of risk and reasonable levels of vigilance, and plan for environmental modification. At-risk individuals may use the information to better understand the magnitude of their own risk (and for what conditions they are at risk), and to plan how to manage and protect their mental health. Other relatives, including grandparents and uncles and aunts, often have similar motivations regarding young, at-risk people in the family. All of these individuals may use the risk information to better come to terms with the illness vulnerability in their family (including from where the vulnerability arose and who is most likely to have the highest risk) and manage the uncertainty that comes with risk.

Effective risk communication requires that you make the information accessible and understandable, and that you assist the client/family member in integrating the information into his or her existing perceptions. Based on the client's or family member's interest and needs, the depth and emphasis of risk communication may vary considerably. Some clients and family members will ask for broad information about the underpinnings of risk for psychiatric illnesses. Others prefer a qualitative discussion of the magnitude of risk. Finally, some clients and family members want the most detailed numerical risk estimation possible. You should be aware that the needs of affected clients and the needs of at-risk relatives may be quite different, both during and after risk communication.

In general, the complexity of discussions about family risk depends on the types of disorders, number of affected individuals, and the quality of the information gathered in the family history. The risk communication may be brief and reasonably straightforward, or it may be lengthy and involve discussions of intricacies, or it may be anywhere in between. We encourage you to refer clients with complex histories or those who request or require additional education and support around risk to a genetics specialist.

You should anticipate that the risk information may evoke strong emotions in many clients, and these emotions may affect their ability to attend to, integrate, and react to the information. Recall that the client's or family member's perception of the illness, risk perception, exposure to affected individuals, and lived experience are likely to affect how he or she responds to the risk information. The client's preconceived ideas about his or her own (or family members') risk status may be based on facts, similarities to or differences from affected relatives, or family or cultural beliefs. Therefore, it is possible that your presentation of risk information may differ from what the client or family member expected. This underscores the importance of beginning the discussion of risk by asking the client or family member about his or her perceived risk. Finally, it is important to remember that it is the client's perception of risks, rather than the "actual risk," that may affect future decisions. You should explore the meaning and interpretation of the presented risks with the client.

Because of the complexity of psychiatric illnesses and our inability to provide unequivocal predictive information about illness in the family, the concept of *managing uncertainty* often becomes a primary focus of interactions around risk. Clients and family members benefit from a discussion of where the uncertainty comes from, how they perceive the uncertainty, and how they can deal with it. Mental health clinicians have asked us if this uncertainty is actually a good reason to *avoid* conversations about family risk, as obviously, we do not want to worry our clients unnecessarily and bring up questions that we, as clinicians, do not feel prepared to fully answer. Though such concerns are natural, you should keep in mind that you are not introducing uncertainty to clients where previously there was certainty. Instead, you are helping your clients address and clarify their current uncertainties about cause and risk. If possible, it can be helpful to provide counseling around the management of uncertainty over multiple sessions to address emerging client needs.

Tips for Incorporating Risk Communication into Practice

You will find it helpful to set the stage early in the process for the inclusion of psychological and emotional issues, fostering discussion of the client's reaction to the information and how he or she plans to use the information. It is important to incorporate information about the client's illness and risk perceptions, values and beliefs, family history, family dynamics, and risk assessment into the discussion.

During risk communication it is important that you provide context for the information. Include a discussion about the population prevalence of the disorder, general concepts regarding the possible contributing factors to the disorder, the concept of *susceptibility* as differentiated from *causation*, the importance of accurate diagnoses, the increased susceptibility to a spectrum of disorders, and the inability to predict which symptoms individuals may develop or how severe those symptoms may be. Discuss frankly our inability to provide completely individualized information about risk and factors that contribute to the development of psychiatric illness.

Risk communication should be a two-way, client-centered discussion between you and your client or family member. Numerical information may be unfamiliar and/or difficult for the client to understand. One way to help with comprehension is to focus on the topics that are considered most relevant by your client. Keep in mind that risk interpretation is a subjective matter, and the client's appraisal of the figures you provide may not be what you expected. For example, whereas some individuals may appraise a 10% chance of developing an illness as being a very low risk, to others this same figure may be appraised as being unacceptably high. It is important to check in to evaluate understanding and provide ample opportunities to let the client discuss perception of risk and response to risk information.

It is important to realize that you do not have to be an expert in risk assessment or risk communication to provide this basic and valuable counseling service. Adjust the amount and complexity of information that you provide based on the client's needs, literacy, and emotional and cognitive status. Keep language as straightforward as possible and reduce or exclude jargon. Consider the subtle intrinsic values embedded in words you use in this context. For example, consider the words *chance* and *risk*. Although both could correctly be used in discussions of family risks for psychiatric illness, we recommend using *chance* instead of *risk* when communicating with clients and family members for two reasons: (1) *chance* is more accessible to clients with lower literacy, and (2) *chance* is a more value-neutral word than *risk*, which connotes a bad outcome.

Even mild to moderate psychiatric symptoms may affect the way that clients attend and respond to risk information. If clients are significantly symptomatic, of course, it is rarely the right time for communication about family risk. You should anticipate that clients who experience greater feelings of stigma, higher perceived burden, and higher perceived risk for recurrence in offspring or other relatives are those who are likely to require more intensive counseling around family vulnerability.

As in other counseling efforts, it is generally more effective to help clients incorporate new knowledge and new ways of thinking about risk into their existing knowledge and perspectives, rather than asking them to replace their existing knowledge and perspectives with the "correct" ones. Keep in mind that clients can hold competing perceptions at the same time (e.g., at different times in your discussion, the same client might say, "I know that it was my terrible upbringing that caused this illness" and "I know that my genes caused my mental illness"). Recall that family members often identify individuals in the family who are perceived as being at higher risk. This attribution of risk may be related to personality factors or risk factors to which the individuals have been exposed; in these cases the attribution might hold some weight because personality factors and environmental triggers may indeed indicate higher risk. In other cases there is less or no validity to these attributions, such as looking like an affected relative or fitting into a particular pattern in the family (e.g., "every third girl in the family is sure to be affected").

Consider using the client's own family history or a risk analogy, such as the "jar model" explained in Chapter 4 to help elucidate the risk discussion. Explain how the client's personal and family history affects how you perceive the applicability of empiric risks. Use the family history to show why empiric risks may approximate the risk magnitude (e.g., no one in the family with very early onset, only one or very few affected relatives, etc.), or why the empiric risk may be an underestimate (e.g., multiple affected individuals in the family). Consider using an analogy like the jar model to reinforce where the risk came from—for example, "Based on your family history, we can see that it is likely that your 'jar' is probably already partly filled with genetic vulnerability."

Finally, reassure clients that you understand how complex this information is and that you are willing to explain things several times and answer any questions. We encourage you to provide the client or family member with a written summary of the risk information. Let the client know that you will be doing so, so that he or she can focus on the discussion instead of trying to take notes or to memorize the information.

Keep in mind that genetic information is family information. It is appropriate to suggest that clients communicate genetic information to interested relatives.

It is important to incorporate psychological support through the risk education and counseling process. Risk counseling often includes identifying psychological and social issues that come about from the client's lived experience and the risk information provided. It is vital that you allow equal time to helping clients process the psychological meaning and implications of the information you are providing. Provide the client with an opportunity to comprehensively consider his or her concerns and questions, whether they are medical, social, psychological, cultural, or spiritual in nature. Additionally, the session should provide insight, guidance, and resources for future consideration.

Anticipate the need for some follow-up after the genetic education and counseling session(s). The initial provision of information may go beyond what a client's current needs or emotional status allows him or her to process. Therefore, the invitation for follow-up appointments is suggested to facilitate further understanding, adaptation, and decision making related to the disorder. It is ideal to check in with the client over time, to see if and how the information about causation and risk has affected his or her perceptions and life plans. For clients who continue to have questions or concerns, consider a referral to a genetics center for genetic counseling (see Chapter 5 for details).

Tips for Incorporating Numerical Risk Assessment into Practice

We have found that there is a great deal of variation in how well individuals understand risk, and comprehension cannot necessarily be assumed based on verbal ability or level of education. It is best to assume that your client/family member needs some assistance with understanding statistics, because many people have a very difficult time understanding numbers and numerical concepts. Following are some tips for providing numerical risks to clients or family members.

• It is not uncommon for individuals to perceive risks from a dichotomous, all-or-nothing perspective (i.e., it *is* or it *isn't* going to happen); it may be difficult for those people to process risks that are presented in a numerical fashion (one chance in ten, or 10%). Check in frequently to assess understanding, and remark that it is only natural that clients should think in terms of "is going to happen versus is not going to happen," since that is the lived truth of the matter— and that it is unfortunate that we are unable to provide definitive information.

• Use different methods to present risk—for example, visual aids, analogies, and written materials. Many clients like very simple charts or graphs. Talk through your risk assessment process.

- When describing risk to clients, provide the population risk as the bottom limit of empirical risk, and discuss it as a comparison point for other risk numbers.
- Use absolute risks as the basis for your risk discussion. Relative risks may be interpreted incorrectly, especially when the disorder is comparatively rare in the general population (e.g., autism). If the client seems to understand the absolute risk, in some cases it may be useful to clarify understanding by comparing the absolute risk to the relative risk.
- Present risks in several different ways, taking clues from your interactions with the client that inform the approaches that you use. We suggest that you begin by presenting the numbers in the form of "out of 100 people with the same level of risk, 25 would become ill" because numbers in this form tend to be the best understood by the majority of people. You may also want to state the same numerical risk as a percentage (25%) or as a fraction (one-in-four chance).
- It is important to frame risks from the perspective of a negative and a positive outcome. For example, after you explain that, if there were 100 people with the same level of risk, 25 would become ill; you could say that this is the same as saying that 75 of the 100 people would not become ill. *Point out explicitly that the majority remains well.* There are very few cases where the family history is significant enough that we would expect the majority of relatives to become ill. If you encounter a case where you suspect that illness onset is more likely than not, based on the family history, consider referring the client/family for a genetics consultation (see Chapter 5 for details).

Tips for Integrating Qualitative Risk Assessment into Practice

Some individuals do not wish to be given a risk number, but instead prefer a qualitative assessment of risk. It is important to be aware of the potential for misunderstanding that comes when using qualitative risk assessment; your own perception of risk level (e.g., very low, low, moderate, high, very high) is very subjective and may be quite different than that of the client or family member. Therefore, the use of such qualitative terms introduces the potential for bias and should be approached with care. If you use such phrases, it is vital to evaluate how the client or family member perceives the phrase.

We find it useful to approach qualitative discussion of risk by stating that risk is increased above general population level and then focus on how relatives are more likely *not* to be affected. (Because most families have only one affected family member, the most appropriate empiric risks are often in the 10–15% range or lower.) For those families, qualitative assessment might be posed as described in the next section.

What You Can Say to Clients and Family Members about Risk Assessment

"What do you think that you might do with the information about risks for family members?"

This is another method of encouraging your client to consider what impact the risk assessment might have for him or her, and it allows you to help the client manage the new information.

"You said that you are interested in hearing about the chances of other family members being affected. Are you interested in hearing specific numbers, or would you like me to talk about it in terms of higher or lower risk than other people?"

This kind of question allows you to tailor the information you provide more precisely to the needs of the individual client, while again preserving the client's right not to know.

"What would be an acceptable level of risk to you, and at what point would you feel that the risk is too high to consider having children?"

It can be important to establish whether this point is something to which the client has given thought, or not. Exploring some of these issues prior to embarking on risk assessment encourages the client to consider potential reactions in advance of receiving information.

"These risk numbers I am talking about come from research studies that have investigated large groups of relevant relatives and disorder; for example, siblings of individuals with bipolar disorder. These studies examine how often the siblings also developed bipolar disorder. Some of the siblings in the research study developed bipolar disorder, some did not. The empiric risk figure is simply the proportion of people in the research group who developed bipolar disorder—so it is an average. It gives us some good information about overall risk in the research group, but it doesn't tell us exactly what the risk of any one person in the group was, and it doesn't tell us exactly what your risk is, either."

Many clients and family members appreciate understanding the source of risk estimates. This is one way in which you might try to explain the concept of empiric risks.

"Your children do have an increased chance of having [the disorder(s) in question]. However, your children have a much better chance of <u>not</u> having it than having it."

Presenting the qualitative information from both angles—both as the chance to be affected and the chance to be unaffected—is an excellent strategy that can be used in the large majority of situations because risk is often estimated at less than 50%.

"Your children do have an increased chance of having [the disorder(s) in question], though it is certainly possible that they will be well. For now, let's focus on the possibility that they

could be affected and discuss [psychological reactions, early intervention, or whatever issue seems most salient]."

For an affected individual who has a family with an unusual number of relatives with psychiatric illness, you might want to consider something like this statement. This kind of statement indicates in broad terms that the chances are likely quite a bit higher than the empirical risk, and it seeks to explore the impact of that information, and/or allow some anticipatory guidance—in the form of perhaps opening a conversation about risk management (covered in more detail in the next chapter).

"Because your family history is a little unusual—you have several affected close family members—and you have said that you would like the most accurate numerical risk estimate possible, I think it might be best for me to refer you to an expert who is better equipped to provide this for you. How would you feel about that?"

Raising the possibility of referral to a specialist for genetic risk assessment (see Chapter 5) is certainly appropriate in situations like this one, where the individual has a significant family history and is asking for the most accurate numerical risk assessment possible.

"It is important to keep these chances in context. The chance for anyone in the general population to develop this psychiatric illness is X in 100."

It is always helpful to return to the point that although the chance for psychiatric illness may be higher for someone who has affected family members, no one has zero empirical risk for psychiatric illness, and that these illnesses are really quite common in the general population.

Issues That Clients and Their Families May Raise

"I'm not worried, because in my family, psychiatric illness skips generations—so because I am affected, my children will be fine."

This is a great example of an idea that it might be helpful to gently challenge. In some cases, you can review the family history with the client and show that the perception itself is incorrect. Alternatively it could be that so far in this family, it does in fact appear that the psychiatric illness "skips a generation." Although this is how the condition has manifested so far in the family, there is no guarantee that this is how it will continue to appear. Again, going through the "jar model" and discussing the causes of psychiatric illness can help demonstrate how an illness can "skip a generation" while the genetic variants that increase risk are nonetheless passed on. The unaffected generation still has genetic vulnerability, but until now, by chance they have not accumulated sufficient environmental vulnerability to manifest illness. There is always a chance that the children of this individual could in fact develop mental illness. This is not going to be a reassuring point for this individual to hear, but it can be helpful to ensure that he or she has correct information available. It will be important to pay attention to the emotions that this type of discussion evokes, and to redirect attention to the fact that the children are more likely to be well than ill. Also point out that this family is well placed to manage any emerging illness well by obtaining the appropriate help and treatment in a timely manner, so as to promote the greatest potential for the best possible long-term prognosis.

"Can you just tell me if I'm right to be worried, instead of coming up with a number?"

No clients should be forced to hear a quantitative risk evaluation if they prefer a qualitative approach, and no clients should be forced to hear about risk at all if they are not emotionally ready for the discussion. Simply express empathy for the client's concerns, and consider that perhaps there is some frustration being expressed, the source of which it might be helpful to identify. Point out that worry depends on far more than simple numbers; instead, it is a product of perceptions regarding severity of illness and the accompanying burden, among other factors. Exploring the reasons for the worry might reveal previously undiscovered information. For example, perhaps this client is so concerned because she thinks that the family member could actually be expressing symptoms of mental illness that he or she has not as yet disclosed. But it is also very possible that the client is simply not comfortable with numbers or finds numerical risk assessment too intimidating.

"I'm concerned about my child, but my pediatrician tells me not to worry, that he's fine."

It could be helpful in this situation to reflect that it is hard to live with the increased chance, to wonder if the behaviors you observe are "normal" or if they may in fact be the first manifestations of mental illness, and to explore in more depth the reasons for the concern about the child in question. If this further exploration leads you to feel that the concern needs to be more thoroughly addressed (e.g., if the pediatrician has no experience with or interest in psychiatric illness and the concerns seem to be well founded), you can gently raise the possibility of a referral to a different mental health specialist to evaluate the child (see Chapter 5).

"I don't understand numbers."

Normalize this experience (most people actually struggle with the kind of numbers involved in risk estimation) and praise the client's honesty. Ask what format might help and suggest some alternatives. For example: *"Would it help if I drew a pie and showed you, as frac-*

tions of the pie, how much chance there was that [the individual being discussed] would have mental illness, and the chance that [he or she] would not have mental illness?" Keep in mind that most clients find natural numbers more accessible than other statistics.

"Why did you tell me that you think my risk to develop psychiatric illness is probably less than the 15% risk I found on the Internet?"

Assuming that the 15% figure is an accurate reflection of the empiric risk data in the literature, explain to the client that the numbers that he or she found on the Internet are *averaged* risks, and that what you have done is to take into consideration the information the client gave you about personal and family psychiatric history to modify that risk for the unique situation. You can explain what exactly it was that made you feel the risk was lower—for example, we know that it is very unusual for people to develop schizophrenia after the age of 50, regardless of whether they have a family history of illness. If the 15% figure does not reflect the information you have about empiric recurrence risks for the illness in question, it can be helpful to point out that although there is a lot of information about genetics and psychiatric illness on the Internet, not all of it is accurate. Consider looking at your client's source to see if it reflects newer information from a reputable source. Explain where you obtained the empiric risk numbers you provided.

Our Experience

We have had numerous experiences with clients or family members who misinterpreted risk numbers. A common example is providing a client or family member with an empirical risk in the range of 15% for a relative to also be affected, and having the client respond with a shocked "Wow, that's much higher than I expected." In some cases the client truly expected a lower risk, and we counsel him or her accordingly, explaining from where we got our risk number and providing psychosocial support. In many cases, however, this common response comes from one of two origins. First, there is a subset of clients who understand the numbers correctly, and appraise 15% to be "very high" as a result of perception of illness severity or burden. For those clients, it is important to validate their concerns and engage in appropriate psychological counseling based on their situation (e.g., their decisions about having children, concerns about existing children or other close relatives, or concerns about their own mental health).

Second, there is a subset of clients who perceive 15% to be "very high" because they do not have a good grasp on numbers. If in doubt, the most helpful immediate response is to turn the percentage into natural numbers and to provide the number not affected as well as the number affected. For example, we'd say, *"Out of 100 people with the same level of risk, 85 will not become affected with the disorder, and 15 will be affected with the disorder."* We often show a picture to help clients understand the proportion affected versus unaffected. After exploring the client's reaction, and especially if we feel that they may not understand the numbers, we might say something like, *"Though the risk is increased, most people with this same risk do not get the disorder."*

Case Example

Clint was a healthy 50-year-old father of two school-age children. He sought genetic risk assessment because he had two siblings who were affected with psychotic disorders. In addition, of his father's sibship of three, only his father was not affected with a psychotic disorder. The same pattern was repeated one generation above, with one unaffected sibling (his great-grandparent) and two affected siblings. Clint reported that he never had any concerns about his own mental health and had experienced no symptoms. He asked for information about the cause of the psychiatric illness and about the risk of his children being affected. I (HP) asked him what he thought the risk to his children to be, and he told me that he though it must be quite significant given the amount of illness in his family. I took a complete family history and used the graphic pedigree to help him appreciate the possible causes for the unusual clustering of illness in his family. I informed him that individuals in his family were at quite a bit higher risk than the average individual and that empirical risks would likely not provide a reasonable approximation of the true risk in his family. We also discussed that his mental health was a very positive sign in terms of risk to his children. I informed him that I placed the risk for his children some-where between the empirical risk (in the range of 3–5%) and 50%, and that I approximated the most likely risk as 15–20% for each of his children. I checked in with Clint several times during the discussion. He clearly understood the information I provided but had difficulty applying the information to his children. I asked him whether my information fit into his thinking that his children were at significantly increased risk, and he informed me that the risk estimate was lower than he expected. After some discussion he was able to articulate that my risk estimate didn't seem to fit into the pattern in his family, in which two of three siblings in each generation were affected. Based on his family history he expected at least one of his children to be destined for illness. I agreed that yes, that had been the pattern to date in his family, but I provided more information about possible etiologies for the illness in his family and helped him understand how the genetic susceptibility factors might have moved through the generations. We discussed how the disorder was not expected to follow the same patterns in subsequent generations and that his history to date was likely a result of chance. My goal was to help Clint achieve a more balanced and less deterministic perception of the risk to his children, including an appreciation that both of his children could remain well.

Case Example

Alexandra was a healthy woman in her late 20s who came for a consultation with her husband. She had a brother with schizophrenia. Alexandra had a 5-year-old son and she was concerned about the risk that her child might develop schizophrenia. She was quite forthcoming about her family history and her concerns about her son, who was exhibiting some mild issues with social maturity. When I (JA) asked Alexandra about her own mental health and that of her husband and his family, she reported no concerns. I pressed Alexandra a bit about her own mental health, explaining to her how important her status was in relation to the risk for her son. She was resistant to any discussion that touched on her own risk of developing a psychiatric illness. She told me that she would have experienced issues by now if she was going to, and she had not come to discuss her risk. By gently pointing out again how important her own mental health was to her son's risk, I was able to engage Alexandra in a limited discussion around her risk, though I assured her that I would not provide her with a risk number if she did not want to receive the information. We spent much of the remainder of the session discussing how difficult it was to have an affected sibling and how important her ongoing mental stability was to her own self-image, though for many years she had harbored secret fears about becoming ill. She agreed to hear more about how her own level of risk and mental health status informed the risk to her son, and I agreed that she was on a very good, stable track in terms of her mental health. She ended up being quite pleased by the likely risk that I provided for her son (assuming that she remained well), stating that it was much less than she had expected.

PART III

TALKING TO SPECIFIC POPULATIONS

CHAPTER SEVEN
_____

Pregnant Women Who Have
a Psychiatric Illness

It is a common public misperception that women with serious psychiatric illnesses do not have children. In fact, most do have children, and many pregnant clients have a variety of concerns about how their illness and treatment may directly or indirectly affect their offspring. In this chapter we address counseling about causes of psychiatric illness and risk when the pregnant individual, or the individual planning a pregnancy, is personally affected with a psychiatric illness. (Although issues about genetics are salient during pregnancy or pregnancy planning for the unaffected relatives of people with psychiatric illness, we deal with this scenario independently in Chapter 10.)

Depending on the psychiatric illness in question, discussions about reproductive planning can be particularly sensitive; in some instances, mental health clinicians are in the conflicting position of having to perform parenting assessments that can ultimately lead to the separation of mother and baby because of concerns about the mother's ability to parent. The difficult and complex issues around mental health and parenting competency are beyond the scope of this book. Instead, in this chapter we simply encourage you to consider how you communicate with clients about reproduction, particularly with those clients who may have a serious psychiatric illness, but whose illness is stable and well managed, and who are doing well. Individuals with a serious psychiatric illness such as schizophrenia or bipolar disorder frequently report being both overtly and covertly discouraged by their clinicians from having families of their own, even if their illness is well managed and stable (Viguera et al., 2002).

The ethos embraced in the field of genetic counseling, which reflects the perspective from which this book is written, is that given enough relevant and understandable information and support, people are capable of making autonomous decisions that are "right" for them based on their own values and experience. In the context of genetic counseling, clients are not advised about whether they should have children. This is not to say that as human beings, genetic counselors do not have opinions on these matters; indeed, we have certainly had consultations during which we had strong personal opinions about what the best decisions were likely to be for a particular client. We firmly believe, however, that promoting and supporting an individual's autonomous decision-making and life planning are our most important roles as genetic counselors.

Sometimes the reasons underlying a clinician's impulse to discourage an individual from having children may be consciously or subconsciously related to the notion that any offspring would almost certainly have the same psychiatric illness. If this is the case, it is worthwhile to remember that:

- The magnitude of risk and the potential severity of illness are uncertain.
- Perceptions of risk and how much risk is acceptable are both highly variable among individuals.
- We are unable to predict, at an individual level, how much family environment and upbringing may affect risk for illness.

Tips for Incorporating Counseling for Pregnant Clients into Practice

As you know, planning a pregnancy or being pregnant often includes concerns about the well-being of the mother and the baby, regardless of the health history of the mother. Women who have a major psychiatric illness may have additional concerns about their mental stability during pregnancy and the postpartum period, the impact of their illness and treatment on their ability to conceive, and the potential effects of medication use during pregnancy on the developing baby. Affected men and women may have concerns about their ability to be effective parents, given their illness and the risk that the baby may eventually have psychiatric illness as well. We encourage you to discuss each of these topics with clients considering pregnancy.

The Client's Mental Health Before Conception, During Pregnancy, and Postpartum

Rarely, you may have the luxury of preconception counseling. This is an excellent opportunity to focus on the importance of maintaining the best possible mental health before, during, and after pregnancy. Anticipate that unsuccessful attempts to become pregnant may affect the individual's mental health, as well as her relationship with her partner, and consider raising this scenario with your client (in a manner that conveys that you are not discouraging her desire for a family, but wish to help her anticipate and plan for different possible scenarios). This point is especially relevant because the impact of some types of psychiatric illness and medications on fertility is uncertain. For example, there is a lower pregnancy rate in women with schizophrenia than in the general population (Haukka, Suvisaari & Lonnqvist, 2003).

There is a common, false perception that pregnancy prevents or minimizes psychiatric symptoms. As you know, symptoms can occur during pregnancy and may have numerous negative consequences, some of them severe. For example, it seems that for a subset of women with schizophrenia, pregnancy may exacerbate symptoms (Solari, Dickson, & Miller, 2009). Further, women with a history of any kind of mood or psychotic disorder have risks for postpartum episodes of depression and/or psychosis that substantially exceed population risks (Howard, 2004). It is important to keep in mind that postpartum psychosis constitutes a medical emergency that requires immediate treatment. It can be important to discuss these issues explicitly with clients who are planning pregnancy and with pregnant clients. Again, remember that these risks should not be considered as precluding the option of pregnancy, but as issues to be factored into the decision-making and planning processes. Table 7.1 summarizes the risks for women with a history of depression, bipolar disorder, or schizophrenia to have postpartum depression or psychosis.

Advance Directives

Even in the context of an interaction that fosters the client's autonomy, you can discuss the potential negative consequences of childbearing, including increased risks for postpartum episodes of illness and associated parenting difficulties. These risks may be minimized through careful advance planning and good social and professional support. Employing these strategies allows many affected individuals to success-

Table 7.1. Risks for Postpartum Depression (PPD) and Postpartum Psychosis (PPP) in Women with Various Personal Histories of Psychiatric Illness

Personal Psychiatric History	PPD Risk (%)	PPP Risk (%)
No psychiatric history	10–15	0.1
Major depression	~25	?
Postpartum depression	~50	?
Bipolar disorder, schizophrenia, schizoaffective disorder	~40	20–30
Postpartum psychosis	?	<90
Bipolar disorder + first-degree relative with postpartum psychosis	?	~75

fully navigate the challenges of pregnancy and parenthood. Pregnancy planning for an individual with psychiatric illness offers you an opportunity to suggest that a group of important friends, family, and clinicians convene with the client to establish advance directives—also known as a Ulysses pact, agreement, or contract—regarding how she would like this group to respond if her mental health deteriorates during the pregnancy or the postpartum period. The name of this kind of agreement refers to the pact that Ulysses made with his sailors so he could safely hear the Siren's song, which was known to cause men to lose their capacity for rational thought. Ulysses told his sailors to plug their ears and tie him to the mast, and under no circumstances to untie him, regardless of what orders he gave under the influence of the Sirens. The idea in terms of pregnancy planning with a woman who has a history of mental illness is much the same—she dictates while mentally well what her wishes would be in relation to her own care and to the care of her newborn in the event that her psychiatric symptoms become problematic, especially if she requires hospitalization. Guidance for completing a Ulysses agreement in the context of psychiatric illness and parenthood can be found at this site: *www.parentalmentalillness.org/Ulysses_tip_sheet.html*.

Use of Psychiatric Medication During Pregnancy

Though women often have visceral negative reactions to the idea of taking medications during pregnancy, the decision about whether a woman should use psychiatric medications during pregnancy is often far from straightforward. Clients tend to have less knowledge about the evidence that untreated psychiatric illness during pregnancy has negative outcomes not just for the mother but also for the fetus (Marcus, 2009). Women's instinctive negative reactions may be exacerbated by having heard about how a few medications have been associated with risks to the fetus. These risks are not associated with all medications, and often the risk of an effect on the fetus is small (in the region of 1%); data about specific teratogenic risks can be found through subscription services such as Reprotox (*www.reprotox.org*) and the Teratogen Information System (*depts.washington.edu/terisweb/teris/*). There is little information available about the teratogenic effects of most psychotropic medications, which puts any clinician in a difficult situation of trying to evaluate risk to the fetus versus benefit to the mother with an incomplete set of data. Keep in mind that many psychotropic medications are excreted in breast milk, and thus it is important to evaluate the risks and benefits of breastfeeding as well (Friedman & Polifka, 1998).

Ideally, decisions about medication use during pregnancy should not be made hastily or based on preconceived notions. Rather, you and your client should collaborate in the process of weighing the risks to mother and fetus of untreated psychiatric illness (if this is something of interest to the client) against the risk of psychiatric medication to the fetus. Decisions for each client should be made on an individual, case-by-case basis, understanding that possible strategies include (1) stopping one or all medications for some of the pregnancy (during the time of highest risk, often the first trimester), (2) stopping one or all medications for the entire pregnancy, (3) changing one or all medications, (4) reducing the dose of one or more medications, or (5) maintaining the same treatment regimen (Yonkers et al., 2009). Consider that the American Academy of Pediatrics recommends that drug treatment is indicated if psychotherapy is inadequate or inappropriate given the patient's severity of illness (AAP Committee on Drugs, 2000).

We encourage you to exploit opportunities that may be available to you in helping women reach the best possible decision for themselves about how to proceed. For example, consider consultation with a specialist in maternal/fetal medicine, a genetic counselor, and/or a psychiatrist with expertise in reproductive mental health. However, we appreciate that some clinicians do not have the luxury of being able to refer their clients for a consultation with a professional who has expertise in the areas of reproductive mental health and the use of medications during pregnancy and lactation. The Appendix lists organizations that offer information and support for both clinicians and clients regarding the effects of medication exposures on pregnancy and lactation.

What You Can Say to Clients and Family Members about Psychiatric Illness, Medication, and Pregnancy

"I appreciate that you told me that you would like to begin a family soon. Let's make a plan that will give you the best chance to have the healthiest pregnancy possible."

Often individuals with psychiatric illness, particularly serious psychiatric illness, are discouraged from having children by clinicians, family members, and friends. It can be a huge relief to have a clinician who responds in a supportive and constructive manner to a disclosure about a desire for children. This does not mean that you should not share concerns, but the concerns should be expressed as part of a supportive discussion focused on solving problems and reducing risk. It can be helpful to explore to what extent the individual feels supported in this desire by friends and family, as often their support is a crucial piece of a successful pregnancy and postpartum plan.

"When planning a pregnancy, it is really important to think about how it might affect your mental health. Would you like to talk about this with me? We could start to make some plans for how we can best maintain your mental health during and after a pregnancy."

This is a good way to open a discussion that might allow your client to share her wishes and beliefs, and it also allows you to address misconceptions. For example, you might find out that the client is not concerned about her mental health during the pregnancy because she has heard that the pregnancy protects against mental health problems, and so she is not planning to take any medications until after delivery. In addition to allowing you to challenge misconceptions and share information, it also opens a space for the introduction of advance directives.

"How do you imagine that you would like to handle medications during the pregnancy?"

As we have seen, decisions around how to manage mental health problems during pregnancy are far from straightforward. The risks to the fetus associated with exposure to psychiatric medications must be weighed carefully against the risks to mother and fetus of untreated psychiatric illness. Despite this need for careful assessment, many women have instinctive negative reactions to the idea of using psychiatric medications during pregnancy. Exploration of these issues early in the pregnancy or in the process of planning a pregnancy allows you to gather detailed information to evaluate the potential benefits and harms, and refer your client to clinicians with specialist expertise, if available and appropriate.

"All women who are considering pregnancy should take folate supplements."

Folate is vitally important during pregnancy for the successful closure of the fetal neural tube and for reducing risks for certain types of birth defects (Alaban, 1999). Even though foods such as bread and cereals often have added folate, it is recommended that women planning pregnancy take additional supplements, usually 0.4 milligrams (mg) daily. Prenatal multivitamins often contain 1 mg of folate. Women on psychiatric medications should talk to their family doctor or psychiatrist about how much folate to take because the recommendations vary for women taking different medications. For example, women taking valproic acid should take 4–5 mg of folate daily (10 times the regular recommended amount) (American Academy of Pediatrics Committee on Genetics, 1999). You should make sure, though, that women taking valproic acid do not misinterpret that advice to mean that they should take four prenatal vitamins a day. Prenatal vitamins contain many different nutrients, some of which can have harmful effects if taken in excess. It is best to begin taking folate at least 3 months before conception, but for women who have not been taking it and who are already pregnant, it is still good to begin as soon as possible.

"Some people who have been diagnosed with a psychiatric illness want to know the chances for their children to develop a psychiatric illness in later life. Is this something that you would be interested in talking about?"

Many clients will appreciate your bringing up this topic for discussion during family planning situations. Some clients would like to know this information but are not sure how to ask the question, have not articulated that desire for knowledge to themselves, or are afraid to ask. This topic is covered in Chapters 2 and 6 of this book. It is always appropriate to refer individuals for genetic counseling, if preferred, to address family risk.

Issues That Clients and Their Families May Raise

"Can I be a good parent even though I have a psychiatric illness?"

You could reinforce the point that people with psychiatric illnesses can be great parents or bad parents, just as those without psychiatric illness can be great or bad parents. Parenting is difficult for everyone, and every parent has his or her own challenges, but there is no reason to think that having been diagnosed with a psychiatric illness would preclude a person from being a good parent. As for all parents, it is good to be aware of and alert to one's own challenges and ready to take action, for example, by having a mental health plan in place such as a Ulysses agreement. Explore the motivation for this question. For example, has this person recently had a conversation with someone who has expressed the view that because of her illness, she could not be a good parent?

"I heard that if you take psychiatric medications during pregnancy, your baby will have birth defects—is this true?"

Explain that for many psychiatric medications there is no evidence of any increased risk of congenital abnormalities (birth defects). For quite a few medications, we do not think that there is much or any risk, but we cannot say for sure. A few medications, though, have been shown to increase risks for certain kinds of congenital abnormalities, though the risk of a baby having one of these problems is still quite small. There is a far greater chance that the baby will *not* have any birth defects even if the fetus were exposed to psychiatric medications in utero. Some women find it helpful to know that many birth defects can be detected during pregnancy by ultrasound. Follow up by asking if the client is pregnant or thinks she may be pregnant; some women have terminated pregnancies because they believed it to be a foregone conclusion that the baby would have birth defects, and so it is important to be especially careful that pregnant clients receive detailed education and counseling so that they make informed choices.

"What happens if I have a relapse while I'm pregnant or in the postpartum period?"

It is helpful to empathize with the fear of becoming symptomatic while pregnant or caring for a newborn. Reassure your clients that you will help them plan ahead to develop the best possible plan for a successful and healthy pregnancy and postpartum period. Validate that these are really important things to be thinking about, and offer to talk together to come up with a plan for how these possible situations should be handled.

Our Experience

Case Example

Mary marched into the genetics counseling room and defiantly introduced herself: "I'm 42, bipolar, single, I don't take medications, and I'm going to get pregnant because I want to have a baby." Mary had been referred by her family doctor. The doctor had strong feelings, which he shared with Mary, that she should not attempt to become pregnant. She told me that their relationship had deteriorated when she stopped taking the lithium he prescribed her, and that he insisted that her illness would not allow her to be a competent mother. She felt he had referred her to me (JA) in the hope that I would persuade her to relinquish her plans for pregnancy through donor sperm. I reflected that I could imagine that she may feel hurt, angry, and disappointed by this kind of response—feelings she affirmed. We talked about her perceptions of others' reactions to her wish to become pregnant. While she had caring friends and family around her, it seemed that they were also not supporting her in this decision. I explained it was not my place to try to persuade her to do—or not do—anything. I told her that I believed that she was the person best able to make the right decisions for herself and that I wanted to make sure that she had all of the information that she might need. At this, any remaining defensiveness evaporated, and she visibly relaxed.

I asked if she had questions about pregnancy-related issues. Although initially she only had one question (about her chances of getting pregnant at age 42), as we talked she came up with more and more questions. She had heard that lithium caused fetal heart defects, so was she right to stop taking her medications before trying to get pregnant? What was the chance she would experience an episode of illness during the pregnancy or afterward? If she made sure that the sperm donor she used had no family history of psychiatric illness, would that prevent the baby from developing bipolar disorder in later life? Over the next 1½ hours, we talked about how it may be more difficult for her to get pregnant at age 42, about the risk to a fetus associated with a mother taking lithium during the pregnancy in relation to the risk of having a baby with a birth defect that all women face, and how risks for some conditions increase as women get older. We also talked about how all women have some risk for developing depression or psychosis during pregnancy or the postpartum period, but how those risks are greater for women who have previously been diagnosed with bipolar disorder, particularly if they are not taking medications. We discussed single parenthood and the importance of support of friends and family.

Based on her family history, we also talked about the chance for a potential child to develop psychiatric illness in later life, assuming she selected a sperm donor with no family history of psychiatric illness. We discussed that the family history provided by sperm donors is limited and is not confirmed by a health care provider, and that even a "perfect" family history report from the sperm donor did not guarantee that he or his relatives would not later develop mental illness.

At regular intervals I checked in with Mary to see how the discussion was making her feel. She told me that it was a lot to take in, and that she realized that there were many factors that she hadn't considered. When she left, she took several informational booklets and accepted the referral I offered for the local reproductive mental health program. I do not know at what decision Mary arrived in the end, but my goal, as I told her, was to provide all the information that she needed, in a supportive environment, to enable her to make the best possible decision. I believe that this is what she did.

CHAPTER EIGHT

Parents of At-Risk Children

In our experience, most clients who are concerned about the potential for psychiatric illness in their at-risk relatives (especially parents concerned about children, and grandparents concerned about grandchildren), and most at-risk individuals who are concerned about their future mental health (especially siblings or children of affected individuals), are very interested in risk-reduction efforts. They tend to express some hope that environmental modification, new treatments, and early intervention may help reduce the risk or minimize the effects of the disorder, but often tell us that they do not know what concrete steps to take to minimize risk. Being at risk, or having children at risk, is intensely worrisome for some clients and family members, and may lead to chronic monitoring of mental status. Anticipate that for parents of at-risk children, discussions about risk reduction may be one of their primary goals. This chapter focuses on the most important and common aspects of these discussions, including parenting and home environment, early symptom identification, other prevention efforts, lack of control over illness onset, and the timing of risk-reduction efforts.

Parenting and the Home Environment

Parents of at-risk children often have concerns about their parenting and may have modified, or plan to modify, their parenting approach or their home environment in an effort to reduce risk of psychiatric illness for their children. For such discussions, it is worthwhile bearing in mind that adoption studies indicate that parenting and home environment do not cause psychiatric illness in the majority of affected individuals (as reviewed in Chapter 1). Although this can be a reassuring message for many parents, the converse is also true. That is, there is also no conclusive evidence about how parenting and home environment can be modified to preclude psychiatric illness onset in the majority of at-risk individuals. It is very important, however, to stress to clients and family members that a stable and supportive home environment is good for the overall mental health and development of any individual. Support clients and family members in active and constructive efforts to improve their parenting approach and home environment, but ensure that they understand that even "perfect" parenting may not preclude the onset of psychiatric illness.

Anticipate that some clients will have concerns about their abilities to parent effectively. Some have concerns that their symptoms will negatively affect their children's upbringing, for example, by producing an unstable and negative home environment when the parent is symptomatic. Clients who themselves have parents who were frequently and severely symptomatic may have concerns about their parenting abilities because they did not have good parenting role models.

Environment and Social Support Outside the Home

As described in Chapter 1, we have learned from adoption studies that nonshared environment seems to play a stronger role in causing serious psychiatric illness than does shared environment. Some portion of this non-shared environment will come from the individual's experiences outside the home. The quality of an individual's social interac-

tions with peers is likely to be both a potential contributing factor
(e.g., good social support systems can serve as a protective factor for
mental health) and an indicator of current mental health (e.g., withdrawal can indicate deterioration of mental health). Keep in mind that
the gene–environment interplay described in Chapter 4 will be at
work: An individual's genes may be influenced by his or her environment; an individual's genes may affect how he or she responds to environmental stimuli; and an individual's genes may affect the sort of
environments to which he or she is drawn. Consider an example of
how this factor may be important in risk-reduction efforts. Say that you
have a client who has major depression. She is concerned about her
teenage son, who is withdrawn and moody. Based on the son's genes,
he may react very poorly to an experience such as being ignored by
his peers. But in addition, the son's genes might also make him less
likely to seek out social interactions by which he can develop a set of
friends. Plus, the fact that he is withdrawn is likely to affect how others respond to him—that hoped-for set of friends might find him un-
friendly and thus make no further efforts to engage him.

Although complicated, this interplay between genes and environment may be amenable to modification and therefore provides several
potential points of intervention. You can encourage parents to be
aware of their children's interactions outside the home. You may want
to encourage parents of young children to help them move into appropriate and stimulating environments. For older children, parents should
be aware of the types and quality of social interactions and the potential for isolation, substance abuse, and other risky behaviors. Encourage parents who are concerned about their children's mental health to
seek professional support for their children.

Prevention Efforts

Early Symptom Identification and Intervention

It is important that you discuss with parents of at-risk children the importance of early detection of psychiatric illness, because early and ap-

propriate interventions improve long-term prognosis (Farooq et al., 2009). Although it may be worrisome to live with risk in the family, a family with affected individual(s) is well placed to recognize symptoms of mental illness very early. Affected individuals and family members are also more likely to be familiar with mental health clinicians and understand how to access mental health services. It may increase clients' sense of control if you highlight and affirm their abilities in this capacity. It can also be helpful to encourage clients to try to reframe some of their worry about increased risks toward feeling empowered and prepared to contribute (by early symptom identification and intervention) to a good long-term prognosis, should symptoms emerge.

You can make sure that clients and relatives understand the range of symptoms that is possible in relation to the disorder(s) in question, and that they understand how early symptoms typically emerge. Especially in families in which a relative has had early onset, it is important to describe the ways that symptoms may emerge in children. Clients are often vigilant about symptoms in their children and may have difficulty determining normal from abnormal behavior. You can offer counseling for such families to help them achieve a balance between appropriate vigilance and inappropriate boundary setting or anxiety. You can also help clients and family members develop a concrete plan for what they will do if they identify symptoms or potential symptoms in the at-risk child.

Other Prevention Efforts

The limited research to date does not indicate clear methods to prevent psychiatric illness. The studies do suggest, however, that there are some steps that at-risk individuals and their family members can take that may be protective.

• Pregnant women carrying at-risk babies should avail themselves of early and complete prenatal care and attend to their health through the pregnancy (Solari, Dickson, & Miller, 2009; Yonkers et al., 2004).

- Some at-risk individuals appear to be more vulnerable after exposure to certain street drugs (most notably cannabis and methamphetamine) and should be educated about the possibility that such substances may trigger episodes of psychiatric illness (Caspi et al., 2005; Degenhardt, 2003). You may want to model for clients and family members how they might approach such discussions with older children and adolescents. (e.g., "Drugs can be bad for anyone. They affect different people in different ways, and because of the problems with mood that we have in our family, they might affect you differently than how they affect other people—and they might be especially bad for you.")
- As is suggested for affected individuals, at-risk individuals can strive for high standards of self-care, e.g., a healthy balanced diet (Amminger et al., 2010), a regular exercise regime (Gorczynski & Faulkner, 2010) and enough sleep (Plante & Winkelman, 2010). Good social supports and the development of strategies to effectively cope with and manage stress may be useful (Alloy et al., 2005; Suto et al., 2009). Of course, it is impossible to maintain a constant and impeccable self-care routine, and it is important that you encourage clients not to feel overly guilty or overly concerned about lapses in self-care, but instead to recognize the self-care achievements that are managed.
- For affected parents with young children, family-based interventions, parenting programs, social support, and day care may help reduce the child-care-related stress for the parents and potentially reduce risk in offspring (Beardslee et al., 2003; Craig, 2004; Lee et al., 2006).

Lack of Control over Illness Risk

Clients with at-risk children and those who are considering having children may benefit from counseling that emphasizes the fact that we have limited ability to protect against the onset of illness in at-risk individuals—a point that may be very distressing to some clients. Education about early symptom identification and risk-reduction efforts, as described above, may help these individuals achieve a higher perception of control.

Timing of Risk-Reduction Interventions

Many parents of at-risk children have questions about the optimal timing of risk-reduction efforts, and unfortunately these questions are very difficult to answer. You can explain that genetic risk is present from the point of conception, and that environmental risk factors may accumulate over time. Different risk-reduction interventions may be most effective at particular times in the lifespan. Adolescence tends to be the most difficult time for parents, as they try to differentiate normal adolescent changes from abnormal behaviors in children who may be approaching the time of highest risk for illness onset. Parents of at-risk children need to understand that the risk for illness onset peaks and then decreases as the children age (see Chapter 5 for more information). Try to maintain a strong focus on the importance of early intervention, empowering parents and other close relatives to identify and seek treatment for symptoms early.

Tips for Incorporating a Discussion about Risk Reduction into Practice

Ask parents of the at-risk child what they think about the likelihood of risk reduction and what efforts they are making in this area, if any. Be aware that they may not have consciously evaluated their actions as related to risk reduction (or not). We have found that it is not unusual for parents of at-risk children to say that they are doing nothing specific to reduce risk, but as our discussion continues, they report a list of ways in which they have modified their parenting approach or home environment. It is important that clinicians reinforce any risk-reduction efforts that parents have undertaken, as well as suggesting other possible efforts.

The parenting/home environment modifications that we hear most often in our counseling sessions include the following:

- Vigilance about the moods and behavior of the at-risk child
- Reducing exposure to stressful experiences, and/or finding more effective strategies for managing stress
- Encouraging the expression of feelings and concerns
- Identifying mental health clinicians and other trusted individuals who can help at-risk children who are going through difficult times or who have questions
- Talking about the importance of abstaining from substance use
- Encouraging good decision making
- Being aware of the child's social network, including whether the child has friends and whether the friends are considered to be positive influences

Expect that many families will be quite pragmatic, hoping to reduce risk but understanding that there should be a strong focus on minimizing symptoms, should they emerge. It is vital to describe the benefits of early intervention and appropriate treatment in long-term outcomes. For many clients, we reinforce this point by contrasting their long road to diagnosis and appropriate treatment to what might have happened if someone close to them had been in a position to notice and act appropriately on their symptons from the start.

Finally, depending on the level of risk involved, for some families you may want to spend a significant amount of time on anticipatory guidance related to the onset of symptoms in an at-risk relative. Such families include those with very high risk—for example, a child with two affected parents, or multigenerational illness on both sides of the family. In these cases, it is especially important that the family has a plan in place for how to deal with emerging symptoms.

We appreciate that your clients may have encountered barriers when attempting some risk-reduction efforts. For example, it can be difficult to get coverage for mental health services for individuals who are exhibiting concerning symptoms but who are still relatively unimpaired, or to get support for affected individuals to attend parenting courses. We hope that you can find creative ways to work with clients and family members so that they have the best chance of accessing care or services that may reduce risk. A final important message to parents of at-risk children is that our understanding of psychiatric illnesses is steadily improving. With those improvements we expect will come new, more targeted, and more effective therapeutics, as well as more definitive diagnoses. It is likely that the outlook for newly diagnosed individuals will continue to improve.

What You Can Say to Clients and Family Members of At-Risk Children

"While your child's chance of developing psychiatric illness is higher than the chance for a child who does not have an affected parent, you actually have one significant advantage over a family who has no experience with psychiatric illness: You know what the symptoms look like. That would allow you to recognize the condition quickly if it did emerge, and get appropriate help. These important actions can improve the long-term prognosis."

Symptom identification and help seeking are important and underrecognized advantages that families with psychiatric illness hold over families that have no such experience. Good evidence is emerging from the literature on early psychosis intervention that the duration of untreated psychosis inversely correlates with long-term prognosis (i.e., the longer the duration of untreated psychosis, the worse the long-term prognosis) (Farooq et al., 2009). In this way, although it may not be possible to prevent the onset of a psychiatric illness, it may be possible to respond to an emerging psychiatric illness in such a way that its impact is reduced.

"Watching your teenager and keeping note of his [or her] moods and behaviors is completely normal. As he gets older, though, how do you think that you'll manage giving him more freedom, while still trying to make sure he stays healthy?"

This is an issue with which most families of at-risk individuals tend to struggle. Opening a dialogue on this topic can allow the client to explore possible plans the family could implement to facilitate the smoothest possible transition for the child into his or her adolescence.

"Have you ever thought about what you would do if you noticed symptoms in your daughter [or son]?"

A statement like this one focuses your discussion on ideas around planning response and management strategies if symptoms do emerge and thereby allows you to provide some anticipatory guidance.

Issues That Clients of At-Risk Children and Their Families May Raise

"If I am a really good parent, can I prevent my child from developing the psychiatric illness that exists in my family?"

After hearing that the environment is an important factor in determing whether someone develops mental illness, people with personal or family histories of mental illness may become attached to the idea that "perfect parenting" can prevent their children from developing mental illness. This would be an important perception to expose and address, as there is no known parenting method by which mental illness can be prevented. On the other hand, "bad parenting" is unlikely to be the sole cause of psychiatric illness. Because parenting approach is the primary aspect through which parents attempt to shape their children's development, clinicians should anticipate that these messages about parenting are likely to challenge parents' perceptions of control. An important message to convey is that "good parenting" will be beneficial to a child regardless of his or her psychiatric status, and should a child become ill, he or she is likely to have a better outcome if he or she has a stable, communicative, and supportive home environment.

"How can I tell if my teenager is OK?"

Reflect that it is difficult to determine the difference between normal adolescent behavior and emerging mental illness, and that managing that uncertainty can be really difficult for family members. You could offer counseling for such families to help them achieve a balance between appropriate vigilance and inappropriate boundary setting or anxiety. Review the manner in which the psychiatric illness(es) for which the young person is at risk may manifest, and to reassure the parent that the teenager is most likely to remain well (if possible and appropriate, given what you know about his or her current mental health status and risk factors).

"She's just a toddler, but I'm already worried about my daughter. How will I be able to stand watching her grow up, just waiting for her to become ill like me?"

Validate this client's concerns, and ask what he or she perceives the risk to be. Ask if the client would like a better understanding of the risk. Ensure that the client understands that his or her daughter is most likely to remain well (if applicable). Understand, however, that his or her concerns may have little to do with the likely quantity of risk, but rather the possibility of any risk at all for the same disorder with which the client lives. Reflect how difficult it can be to live with uncertainty, and help the client determine how he or she will manage it. Explore the client's perceptions of his or her own illness, and explain that if the daughter were to become ill, her experience might be quite different than her parent's. Finally, address the guilt that this client seems to be expressing about passing risk to his or her daughter.

"We have done everything we can to try to make sure that our daughter [or son] stays well."

Support the parents in their efforts to maintain their child's mental health. Ask them about those efforts and how effective they perceive them to be. Help them understand and manage their inability to prevent the illness while reinforcing the fact that they may be effectively reducing the risk through their efforts. Clarify that we simply do not know how to significantly reduce risk and reinforce your perspective that their efforts seem constructive (if applicable).

"If I make sure he [or she] stays away from street drugs, he'll be fine, right?"

Help clients understand that limiting exposure to a potential environmental "trigger" is helpful, but because so many factors can contribute to development of psychiatric illness, not all of which we can control like this, we cannot prevent illness. Address how emotionally challenging it is to be unable to control whether an at-risk person will develop a psychiatric illness.

Our Experience

Case Example

Bill was a 75-year-old man diagnosed with bipolar disorder who wanted to know more about the chance that his daughter would be affected with a mood disorder. His daughter was in her early 20s, and Bill described all of the efforts that he and his wife had made to try to ensure that she did not experience any environmental conditions that might further increase her chances of developing bipolar disorder. They tried to create a calm, safe, and supportive home environment, and they taught their daughter how to make "good" decisions. They tried to always be available to their daughter if she needed to talk about her feelings or if she wanted their opinions.

Bill had a few symptomatic periods during his daughter's childhood, and though he thought they were undoubtedly disruptive and scary for her, he felt that he and his wife had done as good a job as they could with providing age-appropriate information and shielding her from as much as possible. As she got older, Bill had several very general discussions with her about his illness. Bill wanted some guidance about how to have a much more frank and detailed discussion now that she was an adult, including how to talk to her about her own risk for bipolar disorder. He also wanted to know if there was anything else that he could be doing to further reduce her chance for the disorder.

I (HP) spent some time describing the etiology and likely risk, and Bill practiced how he might present the information to his daughter. In terms of prevention efforts, we discussed how avoiding street drugs would certainly be something that could protect her mental health. I also described the importance of early symptom identification and early intervention. Though he could not control his young-adult daughter's exposure to risk factors, he could discuss his own experience, model open communication about his own mental health, describe the importance of asking for help, and inform his daughter about the potential effect of street drugs. Bill had not considered how early intervention might impact his family, if the "worst" did happen and his daughter developed bipolar disorder. When I presented this as an option for discussion it was enthusiastically accepted, and Bill left telling me that he felt somewhat more hopeful about his daughter's future.

Case Example

Miles was a 40-year-old man diagnosed with obsessive–compulsive disorder (OCD). He and his wife Tanya attended genetic counseling because his wife was concerned about their three children's risk to also become symptomatic of OCD. The children ranged in age from 4 to 12. Miles was clearly upset with Tanya and immediately explained that this was all her idea—he did not want to attend the appointment and only came because his wife insisted. I (HP) explored their risk perceptions, which were quite different. Miles initially insisted that his children were at no risk because the disorder "skips generations." Tanya thought that their risks were maybe about 50%—something she had read on the Internet. This was a complicated case because each parent had strongly-held perceptions, and they were quite different. I asked each to listen carefully to the other's perspective.

Miles stated that he and his wife had raised his children in a supportive, active, and stimulating environment. This environment was nothing like the one in which Miles had been raised, which was strict and emotionally cold. Miles also pointed out that all three children seemed to have personalities that were much more similar to Tanya's than to his own. He took that as another sign that they were not at risk; it was clear that he used these attributes to distance his children from any risk. Miles's wife expressed significant frustration with this discussion. She wanted Miles to see that these things might be positive, but they did not mean that the children had no risk. She asked many questions about the potential benefits of additional environmental modification, ignoring Miles's obvious discomfort. Miles was as frustrated with Tanya, because in his view she seemed to expect their children to become affected. In addition, Miles felt that his disorder was quite manageable and not that disruptive to his life, while Tanya felt that it had significantly affected his employability and social life. It was clear that these issues would not be resolved during a single session. I reinforced the point that their healthy home environment, as described by Miles, was certainly beneficial to their children's development, whether they remained healthy or became symptomatic. I educated them about the etiology and the likely risk based on their personal and family histories, taking care to ask each to verbalize how he or she perceived the risk. I stated that the issue of risk to their children was clearly important to both of them but that they were far from finding common ground, or even seeing merits in each other's positions. Thus I suggested a referral to a marriage counselor to help the couple deal with the issue and invited them to re-contact me for additional education and genetic counseling.

CHAPTER NINE

Parents of Affected Children

Having a child develop a major psychiatric disorder is usually an intensely distressing experience for parents, regardless of whether it is a childhood-onset disorder or a disorder that emerges during adolesence or young adulthood. When children become ill, anticipating and responding to parents' questions such as "Why my child?" and "What could I have done to prevent this?" require careful attention to both education and psychological support. This chapter builds upon the advice in previous sections of this book and provides guidance when educating and counseling parents or guardians of affected minors.

In this chapter we focus on the autism spectrum disorders (ASDs) and the pediatric onset of psychiatric disorders that typically have adult onset (though the concepts we present apply to other psychiatric disorders in children). These groups of disorders tend to require significant parent education and psychological support. In addition, we recommend that you consider a referral to a genetics specialist for ASDs and pediatric-onset mood and psychotic disorders.

Autism Spectrum Disorders

ASDs present specific challenges to mental health clinicians who are providing education about factors that contribute to the development of illness and family risk. As you are probably aware, the rate of diagnoses of ASDs has increased quite significantly over the past 10 years. Recent reports posit that the prevalence of autism spectrum disorders is 1/100 (*www.cdc.gov/mmwr/preview/mmwrhtml/ss5810a1.htm*). The exact cause of this increase is not yet known. Experts disagree about whether the frequency of the condition itself is on the rise, or whether the frequency of the condition itself is stable but a greater proportion of affected children are receiving appropriate diagnoses. The causes of autism have been a matter of intense public interest and debate, and much misinformation exists, including the common misperception that increased vaccine exposure has caused the increased rates of autism. Several studies, as reviewed by DeStefano and Thompson (2004), have concluded that vaccines did not cause autism in the large majority of clients (though it is possible that exposure to vaccines does trigger symptoms in a small percentage of genetically vulnerable individuals). As in other major psychiatric illnesses, research suggests that for most affected individuals, genes and environment interact to cause symptoms.

As with other major psychiatric illnesses, relatives of individuals with ASDs are at increased risk for psychiatric disorders. The empiric risk for autism in a child with an affected sibling is approximately 5–10%, with risks at the higher end of the range if the affected child is a boy and at the lower end if the affected child is a girl. If two siblings are affected, the empiric risk for another sibling increases to about 25–35% (Miles et al., www.GeneReviews.org, accessed 2010). We have less data for other ASDs, but it is expected that the risks are similar. Data also suggest that relatives of an individual with an ASD have increased risk for a range of ASDs and other milder, related manifestations (Schaefer & Mendelsohn, 2008; Szatmari et al., 2000). In addition, mood disorders and anxiety disorders are more common in close relatives (Bolton et al., 1998; Mazefsky, Folstein, & Lainhart, 2008). As with other psychiatric illnesses, it is also not uncommon to hear of relatives who have some features of the condition, but who are able to function completely normally. For example, parents of a child with autism might describe relatives who have awkward social interactions or who are "brilliant eccentrics."

All children diagnosed with autism should be referred to a pediatric geneticist for an evaluation. Following the tiered evaluation scheme recommended by Schaefer and Mendelsohn (2008), it is expected that a clinical genetic examination and genetic testing will identify a genetic cause in about 15% of affected children—and this number is expected to increase as new genetic tests become available. When autism is associated with a genetic syndrome, risks for recurrence in close relatives may be quite different than that predicted by empiric risks, and in many cases prenatal testing or testing in very young siblings is possible. In addition, when autism is associated with a genetic syndrome, there are often also other associated health risks and knowledge of these risks may affect medical management.

Finally, the emotional and practical burden of autism and other severe developmental disorders make it vital that clinicians attend to parents' feelings about their children and themselves. Many parents feel at least partially responsible for their children's illness. This may be especially true in families where the parent or other close relatives have mild symptoms or mood disorders that the family perceives as related to the illness in the child. Parents who choose to have additional children may have serious concerns about younger siblings and benefit from education about risk and counseling about their uncertainty and anxiety.

Pediatric Onset of "Adult" Psychiatric Disorders

As described in Chapter 5 (on risk assessment), pediatric or early teen onset of mood or psychotic disorders indicates a greater genetic contribution to illness, and risk for close relatives to also be affected is increased. In this type of situation it is important to educate parents about factors that can contribute to the development of psychiatric illness and reinforce the message that parenting and home environment did not cause the illness. Given the increased rate of illness in close relatives, be aware of the chance that one or both of the parents might have challenges to their own mental health. If there are concerns about the parents' mental health, addressing those concerns might allow the family to better cope with the illness in the child.

Pediatric diagnosis of mood and psychotic disorders has also been associated with a more severe illness course (e.g., children with bipolar disorder have much higher rates of rapid cycling and increased rates of comorbidity) (Smoller & Finn, 2003). Children often have secondary developmental problems that result from their illness, including poor peer interactions and delayed social development (see Rapoport, 2000). Diagnosis and treatment of these disorders are often difficult. Parents, siblings, and other caregivers require a great deal of education and psychological support.

Parents who have attempted to give their affected child a stable upbringing should be encouraged to reframe feelings of failure and instead recognize that they provided a strong base that will allow the child and family to more successfully meet the challenges of a psychiatric illness. There is some evidence that relapse rates of some psychiatric illness are higher in families with high "expressed emotion," or high levels of criticism, hostility, and emotional over-involvement (Hooley, 2007). Although it is difficult to identify definitively anything other than a correlation between the high expressed emotion and relapse, it makes intuitive sense that helping families to communicate more effectively and cope better with the illness may help support the whole family and potentially reduce the rate of relapse in affected individuals.

When a close relative has been diagnosed with childhood onset of a mood or psychotic disorder, it is important to educate adult relatives about the presentation of emerging symptoms, especially how those symptoms might look different than those in an adult (e.g., irritability in a depressed child). Early symptom identification and early intervention may help reduce the effect that the symptoms have on the child's social and emotional development.

Finally, we recommend the adoption of a low threshold for referral to a genetics specialist when a client has an early onset of illness; when in doubt, refer! It is always appropriate to consult with a genetics professional when an affected child has developmental delays or birth defects, or a family history of developmental delays or birth defects, or if the child has a strong family history of psychiatric illness.

Tips for Incorporating Education for Parents of Affected Children into Practice

Counseling and support for parents' day-to-day caregiving responsibilities for their affected children must remain the top priority, but you may find it effective to incorporate education about the factors that can contribute to the development of psychiatric illness and concerns about risk in a holistic manner. It is important to focus on the entire family when counseling parents who have affected children. This is true for diagnosis and treatment planning, and it is also true for education and risk counseling. The diagnosis of any psychiatric illness in a child often raises intense concerns about recurrence in siblings, and often has strong effects on decisions to have subsequent children. If you care for children who have psychiatric diagnoses, you should be prepared to help the parents of these children make informed reproductive decisions. These families may also appreciate your assistance with understanding and managing the level of risk to siblings and the associated uncertainty and waiting time as they watch younger siblings grow.

As described above, parental guilt and sense of responsibility for the illness in affected children may be more intense than for adult-onset disorders. Parents may feel that there is a public perception that they are responsible for the disorder in their child. As you know, though trying to "talk parents out of their guilt" is ineffective and may in fact be counterproductive, you should aim to normalize their feelings and ensure that they have a reasonable understanding of the cause of the illness.

When a diagnosis occurs notably earlier in life than is typical for that illness (e.g., childhood-onset schizophrenia), the inference made by those with a genetics perspective is that this likely occurs because the individual has a relatively greater contribution of genetic vulnerability to illness. You can use the "jar model" described in Chapter 6 to help explain to parents that an individual who experiences childhood onset is likely to have a jar that includes more genetic vulnerability. A jar that starts out with more genetic vulnerability is more likely to reach fullness (at which point the individual experiences active mental illness) at an earlier age. Similarly, you can use the jar model and the family history to explain that because the affected individual is likely to have more genetic vulnerability, his or her relatives are likely to be at higher risk for illness compared to relatives of an individual who experienced adult onset.

What You Can Say to Parents of Affected Children

"Can you tell me your thoughts are about what caused this illness in your child?"

A statement or question along these lines can be really helpful in gauging the parents' views on the causes of the illness in their child. This can serve as an entry into explorations of any feelings of guilt and anger related to the origins of illness, and can also lead to discussion about what is known about the factors that contribute to the development of these illnesses.

"Are you concerned about your other children?"

Asking about this issue directly will be welcome by some parents. For those who have more than one child, the thought of onset in other children may be associated with so much fear that it is very difficult to acknowledge the question, let alone verbalize it. For these individuals, having you pose the question might feel like a real relief. For others, however, it may be too difficult to consider and the question may be met with an angry/upset response. In these cases, some parents may need more time to adjust to having an affected child before they discuss risk to their other children, and some parents will never be interested in discussing risk to other children. Nevertheless, the fact that you have broached the topic should indicate to them that you are willing and able to support them around this difficult issue, and so lays the foundation for future discussion.

"Do you plan to have other children?"

You should consider addressing this important question to parents who are still in their childbearing years. The diagnosis of the family member can dramatically impact future childbearing decisions. A parent's perceptions of risk for additional children to be affected might be quite different from the empiric risks. If parents are interested, referral for genetic counseling is appropriate because the estimation of risk for relatives is complicated by the young age at illness onset, and the need to rule out genetic syndromes.

Issues That Clients and Their Families May Raise

"Did I somehow cause this?"

If a parent of an affected child asks this kind of question directly, it is especially important to provide a definitive and emphatic response that he or she did not and could not have caused the illness. You should also point out that we do not yet have firm insights about methods that could have been employed to prevent it. Just as it is important to be clear and emphatic with this initial answer, it is equally important to explore the motivation for the question and examine issues around feelings of guilt and responsibility.

"Can I prevent my next child from having autism by having a girl?"

The simple answer to this question is no. It is important for the parent posing the question to understand why this is the case. The relative risk for autism in boys and girls depends on the cause of the autism (see Chapter 5). In the most common cases of autism, though the chances for autism are lower for girls than boys, girls can still be affected. Some parents may be considering options such as sperm sorting to dramatically increase the chance for a female fetus, or early prenatal diagnosis with termination of a male fetus. It is vital that they understand that having a female baby does not guarantee a healthy child. We recommend referral to a genetics professional for a consultation about these issues.

"Can I tell during pregnancy if my next baby will have the same disorder?"

The answer to this question may be quite complex. If the childhood-onset illness in question is related to the presence of a genetic syndrome (as can be the case for about 15% of individuals with autism), then it may be possible to perform a test during the pregnancy that would indicate whether the fetus had the same genetic syndrome. It is more likely, however, that the psychiatric illness is not related to the presence of a genetic syndrome. At present, in those cases it is not possible to test a fetus for the illness. Again, a thorough response to this question would necessitate inquiring into the motivation for the question.

"If my other child makes it through her teenage years without developing the mood disorder that her brother has, is she going to be OK?"

You can assure this parent that the older her daughter becomes without experiencing any mood symptoms, the less likely she is to develop a mood disorder. However, it would also be important to point out the typical age range for onset of the disorder. Even if the affected brother had early onset, this does not necessarily mean that the daughter would have early onset as well. While emerging from the teenage years unaffected is a hopeful sign, she would not quite be out of the period of highest risk. It is also important to inform the parent of the prevalence of major depression, especially the increased prevalence in women, regardless of family history.

Our Experience

Case Example

Drs. Anderson—she a pediatrician and he a radiologist—attended genetic counseling because they were expecting their second child, and their first child, Mark, was 4 years old and diagnosed with autism. They explained that they were interested in receiving the most up-to-date and comprehensive information possible about the etiology of their son's autism and a quantitative assessment of risk to the pregnancy. Their son had recently been evaluated by our genetic center's medical geneticist, who was unable to identify a syndromic etiology for the disorder. The couple eloquently described how difficult it was not to latch on to "fad explanations" for their son's illness because they were so desperate to know what had caused the autism and to reduce some of the guilt that they felt about his illness. They appreciated that their medical backgrounds allowed them to evaluate the literature on possible causes, including vaccinations, but they were frustrated that every possible explanation seemed like a dead end. I (HP) explained the current understanding of the etiology and, given their backgrounds and training, provided the couple with some relevant review articles from the medical literature. I described the natural reaction of parents to feel guilty when they have affected children. Mrs. Anderson reflected that she often saw this reaction in her pediatric practice even when there was no blame to be placed, as in her situation. I later asked them about their risk perceptions for the developing baby. They had a reasonable understanding of the empiric risk for recurrence of autism. Mr. Anderson told me that the pregnancy was "not really planned"; they had decided not to risk having another child, but both had really wanted another baby, and they were pleased but worried about this pregnancy. The couple was scheduled to have an ultrasound the following month, and Mrs. Anderson expressed her strong hopes that the baby would be a girl. She understood that having a female may reduce but would not negate the increased risk caused by their family history. I continued the session by engaging the couple in a discussion about how they would manage the uncertainty about whether the baby would be well for the rest of the pregnancy and early in the baby's life. The couple left the session with a more nuanced understanding of the etiology of autism and the risk to their pregnancy.

Case Example

Rosa and Thomas were referred to genetics counseling by their child's psychiatrist. Lily, age 11, had been diagnosed about 6 months previously with bipolar disorder. The couple arrived at the session saying that they were happy to learn more about their daughter's illness, but that they were unclear about the goals of the session. I (JA) told them some of the possible topics that we could discuss, but asked them to begin by sharing their family story with me. They shared a long, heart-wrenching tale of their daughter's symptoms, which began about 4 years before her diagnosis; their quest for a diagnosis and effective treatment; and the impact of her illness on her sister and the family.

They described Lily as an active, imaginative, social child who had transformed into a frequently irritable, violent, and hypersexual pre-teen. During this tale, Rosa frequently asked if it was OK that they were talking so much. When I assured her that this was a confidential and safe place to describe their experiences and that I was here for them, Rosa stated that she was just so grateful to finally be able to get share the experience, to "get it off my chest." Thomas agreed that telling the story was cathartic. I reflected what a tremendously large burden this experience had been on the family, and we discussed the potential benefits of therapy for the couple.

I later took a family history and provided information about the likely etiology of Lily's illness, and then we discussed the couple's concerns about their other daughter, Claire, age 14. Thomas stated that he was glad that Claire was older than Lily because otherwise he would be terrified that she would also become ill. We discussed her likely risk and the range in ages at onset. The couple was reassured by what they perceived as a low risk to Claire. I asked them how much they had shared with Claire about Lily's illness, and they said that they wished that they could tell her more, but that they could never find the right way to describe Lily's diagnosis. I suggested that they do some role playing with me to explore different ways of describing Lily's illness to Claire, and they readily agreed, with good results. Finally, our discussion moved back to their expectations for Lily and their hopes for more symptom stability in the near future.

CHAPTER TEN

Unaffected Family Members

For unaffected family members and spouses of affected individuals, common issues that could effectively be addressed by providing education and support about the causes of psychiatric illness include the following:

- Concerns about whether they could have prevented the illness or had done something to cause the illness in their relative
- Fear about becoming affected themselves in the future
- Concern about their own *current* mental health status
- Choosing not to have children or feeling that they should not have children because of fears that the children would be affected too
- Feeling "different" from other families who don't have a member with psychiatric illness

Although any relative of an affected individual could need education and counseling about his or her family member's illness, as we have already discussed some of the concerns of parents of affected and at-risk children, in this chapter we focus on how to provide education and counseling about genetics and psychiatric illness for siblings, children, and spouses of affected individuals. As a mental health clinician, you are most likely to come into contact with the immediate family members of affected individuals, and they are the group that is most likely to need support around these issues.

Family support seems to be an important factor in recovery and in relapse prevention for individuals with psychiatric illness. With early psychosis intervention programs (which evaluate and treat individuals with early manifestations of psychosis in an effort to attenuate it as quickly as possible, and in so doing, potentially improve long term prognosis) leading the way, mental health care is increasingly embracing the concept of working with family units rather than individuals alone. In these and similar programs, mental health clinicians may come into contact with unaffected spouses, siblings, and children of their clients. Spouses, siblings, and children often report feeling excluded from discussions with clinicians about their affected relative, and because they are unlikely to be in the care of a mental health clinician themselves, they may have not have access to a professional who can answer their questions about causes of illness and family risk.

Because family support is so important in recovery and relapse prevention, addressing some of these concerns could potentially help their affected family member indirectly. By supporting the child/sibling/spouse, he or she may in turn be better able to support the affected family member.

Tips for Incorporating Education of Unaffected Family Members into Practice

In our experience, children and siblings of affected individuals often have strong fears about their own mental health, both current and future. They may feel "destined" for illness. Many describe being hypervigilant about their mental health, constantly checking their perceptions and moods. These at-risk children and siblings greatly benefit from discussions about factors that contribute to the development of illness and risk. Indeed, many of them tell us that no one has been willing to listen to their concerns and their experiences living with an affected relative, and that being willing to bear witness to their stories is a great service to them.

In discussions with siblings and children of affected individuals about reproductive decision-making, keep in mind that at-risk women also have increased risk for postpartum illness. It can be helpful to educate women about the symptoms of postpartum depression or psychosis (as relevant, based on their family history) and counsel them to inform their obstetrician or midwife about the increased risk.

Spouses and significant others are often very motivated to understand the cause of illness in order to better understand and best help their partners. They may also harbor fears about the risk for their children/potential children to develop the same illness as their partner.

It is important to recognize that close relatives of individuals with psychiatric illnesses may be affected by the associated stigma. This kind of stigma expressed toward family members has been labeled "courtesy stigma" (Angermeyer et al., 2003), because the negative attitudes toward affected individuals are extended to (i.e., courtesy) close relatives or friends of individuals with psychiatric illness. The extension of stigma may stem from ideas of contagion (i.e., illness "rubbing off"), "birds of a feather" (i.e., that individuals who have close relationships with people with psychiatric illness must themselves be unstable), or notions of predisposition (i.e., that relatives of individuals with psychiatric illness are genetically and/or environmentally predisposed to illness). When talking about the causes of psychiatric illness, it is vital to talk about the shared role of genetics and environment, instead of about one or the other exclusively. It is possible that educating clients, relatives, and the public about the complex nature of the causes of psychiatric illness—with a message that the types of factors that contribute to the onset of psychiatric illness are very similar to those of other common diseases, such as heart disease and cancer—may reduce illness-related stigma (although this impact remains to be determined).

Alternatively, unaffected relatives may not experience discrimination, but rather may perceive others to view them negatively, or perceive themselves as being less valuable because they have an affected family member. Devaluation of the self in this way amounts to internalized stigma, which may be associated with the greatest negative outcomes (Ritsher & Phelan, 2004). Hopefully, however, it may also be the facet of stigma that is the most amenable to modification. Although it is proving difficult to change society's attitudes toward psychiatric illness, it may be more achievable to influence how someone feels about him- or herself as a result of having an affected family member. Discussion of the factors that contribute to the development of psychiatric illness and family risk with unaffected relatives may bring these issues to the surface, and you are well placed to help the unaffected relative with them.

What You Can Say to Unaffected Family Members

"The bulk of the attention has been on your sibling [parent/ spouse], but I know that this must be affecting you deeply too. Are there questions or worries that you have that I might be able to help with?"

This sort of overture might come as a surprise, so particularly for teenage children/siblings, encourage them to think about the offer and check in with them again. Provide them with your card and an invitation to contact you if questions or concerns arise.

"It can be really frightening to see someone you love go through all of this."

A statement like this one can open the door for relatives to tell you about how they experience their family member's illness, and perhaps even express concerns about, or appreciation of, their own mental health.

*"When people have a parent [sibling] with a condition like this,
they might worry about whether they are somehow responsible
for the illness."*

This can be a very delicate but very important topic that is often difficult for people to verbalize themselves, but can be associated with significant distress. A statement like this can be a great opener to a more complete exploration of beliefs and misconceptions about illness causation. You can follow with a discussion about what is known to contribute to the development of psychiatric illnesses in a way that may allow for a reduction in self-blame and distress.

*"Sometimes family members worry about their own mental
health and/or their children's mental health when a loved one is
diagnosed."*

It can be helpful for people who are struggling with these issues to recognize that these are normal concerns. This type of statement could initiate a conversation about the individual's current mental health concerns, fear about future psychiatric illness, fears about existing children, or even worry that future parenthood is not a responsible option because of the illness in the family.

Issues That Unaffected Family Members May Raise

*"How can I know whether I will develop a psychiatric illness like
my sibling [parent]?"*

You can reflect that it is a normal response to have these worries under the circumstances, explore the current degree of distress, and ask whether there are any current symptoms that have prompted the family member's concern. Assuming that the individual is not symptomatic, it is appropriate to share with him or her that, at present, there is no way to know for sure whether he or she will develop psychiatric illness. You could acknowledge that it can be very difficult to live with this uncertainty. It is important to ask the family member whether he or she is interested in more information about risk based on his or her medical and family history, and to provide a risk assessment or refer for risk assessment. Make sure to emphasize that the chance that he or she will not develop psychiatric illness is greater than the chance that he or she will become ill (as applicable; there are rare exceptions, including for an identical twin of an individual with schizophrenia or bipolar disorder). You can also discuss efforts the client can implement to protect his or her mental health.

"I couldn't watch a child of mine go through what my spouse [parent/sibling] has gone through, and I imagine that he or she would likely have this illness too, so I guess I just better not have kids, right?"

Many people who do not have psychiatric illness themselves but who have an affected family member overestimate the risk for their own children to develop psychiatric illness. In fact, it seems that some percentage of unaffected family members of people with psychiatric illness choose not to have children at all, based in part on this overestimation of risk (Austin, Smith, & Honer, 2006). In this situation, it would be very appropriate to acknowledge how difficult it is to watch a loved one struggle in this way, and to offer to sit down to discuss how these illnesses arise because that might help the individual to understand what the chance might be for potential children to develop the same illness.

Our Experience

Case Example

Brian and I (JA) were making small talk at a social function, where we had just met. When he asked what I did, I replied that I was a genetic counselor who was specifically interested in providing services for people with psychiatric disorders, such as schizophrenia and bipolar disorder, and for their families. Brian told me how interesting he thought that was, and explained that his wife, to whom he had been married for more than 20 years, had been diagnosed with bipolar disorder. He then told me that they had recently divorced after he attended a public lecture about bipolar disorder where the presenter had talked about how the condition was "mostly genetic." When Brian heard this, he told me that he felt that because her condition was "genetic" her fate was set, and that since there was no hope she would ever recover, it was best that they divorce. This interaction made me appreciate even more poignantly the impact that messages around the issue of psychiatric illness causation can have. Although I had not been the presenter in question in this instance, I reflected on how careful I have to be with language when discussing these issues, and that I have to make sure that I am alert to recognizing and responding to the immediate reactions people have to the information I provide.

Case Example

Paul's father and a paternal great-aunt had been diagnosed with bipolar disorder. Paul was in his mid-30s, and he had been worried about his own mental health for as long as he can remember. He constantly checked his own emotions and was concerned that any ups or downs might indicate the onset of a mood disorder. Lately, Paul was beginning to think that he might have escaped from the illness; he correctly understood that he had less risk for onset of the disorder as he got older. In the past month, however, Paul's 38-year-old sister was diagnosed with major depression with psychosis. The diagnosis shocked Paul and greatly increased his concern. He was very close to his sister and always thought that she was the "strong one" in the family. He felt that his understanding of the disorder risk must be wrong if his "strong" sister had become affected at such a late age. We discussed the disorder etiology and how it can cluster in families in unpredictable patterns. I (HP) reinforced his understanding that risk is reduced with age, but we discussed the wide range of onset ages for mood disorders. We explored what it meant to be "strong" in Paul's family and discussed that having a psychiatric illness does not mean that Paul's sister is weak. We discussed Paul's own risk, his mental status, and how he can live with the continued uncertainty about his own mental health.

CHAPTER ELEVEN

Talking to Clients About Genetic Susceptibility Testing

This chapter reviews basic principles and points for you to consider when you counsel clients about testing for genetic susceptibility. It is important to appreciate that there are different types of genetic testing, and those types have different capabilities, limitations, and implications for clients and their family members. The clinical usefulness of different types of genetic testing varies considerably, as does the ability to predict the outcome under study. Most uses of genetic testing in the psychiatric context (with the exception of genetic testing for a single-gene cause of rare syndromic presentations of psychiatric illness) are best considered as emerging technologies—that is, in certain cases they may provide very useful information, but the best use and interpretation of such tests are subject to debate. As our knowledge increases, so will our ability to inform client care with many types and uses of genetic testing.

Investigating genetic susceptibility to psychiatric illness is a very active area of research, and new study findings are published every week. As such, it is largely impossible for most busy mental health care clinicians to stay abreast of ongoing developments in this field. It may be reassuring to know that, despite the fact that there will be changes over time to the scientific evidence regarding specific genetic variations that may confer vulnerability to psychiatric illnesses, our basic understanding about etiology and our perceptions about what is needed for a genetic test to achieve clinical utility are unlikely to change.

As we have described throughout this book, psychiatric illness arises as a result of the combined effects of genetic and environmental susceptibility factors, and the relative contributions of genetic and environmental vulnerability are likely to vary between affected individuals. Although the details about specific genes that confer susceptibility may change over time, a core message is that the necessity of environmental risk factors in illness causation and the heterogeneity of the factors that contribute to the development of illness between affected individuals make it most unlikely that any single genetic test will ever be able to accurately predict who will and will not develop mental illness. Because of the role of the environment, the best that genetic susceptibility testing will be able to offer, at least in the majority of cases, is probabilistic information (i.e., whether and how much an individual's risk to develop a particular psychiatric illness is elevated above the population level). At present, most individual genetic variations that have been implicated in psychiatric illness confer increases in risk that are so small that testing for them would not motivate any different course of action (e.g., prophylactic treatment) for an individual who was found to carry one. In addition, little is known about how different combinations of genetic variations interact with each other to impact overall risk. Thus, there are currently no genetic tests that have been agreed upon by the scientific community or approved by any professional or federal body as having clinical validity or utility for determining susceptibility to psychiatric illness.

Despite these caveats, it is still possible to send a sample of one's DNA for such testing, which is offered by several Internet-based companies—an area of business practice that currently lacks substantive regulation. It is possible, then, for your client and/or their family members to access genetic testing for susceptibility to psychiatric illness—albeit testing that is neither well validated nor of accepted clinical utility. A number of research studies have been conducted in which researchers present hypothetical genetic testing situations to individuals with psychiatric illness and their relatives. These studies indicate that this population is interested in the prospect of genetic susceptibility testing for psychiatric illness, especially as the predictive power of the hypothetical genetic testing increases. This population has a strong interest in using this kind of testing for themselves and their children, and to a lesser degree, for prenatal genetic testing to determine whether a fetus is at increased risk for psychiatric illness (Jones et al., 2002; Meiser et al., 2008; Trippitelli et al., 1998). What remains unknown is why such testing is of interest; specifically, what would affected individuals and/or their family members do with the information?

Evaluating Genetic Susceptibility Testing for Incorporation into Practice

Though the concept of genetic susceptibility testing is exciting, it is important not to overstate its potential. As a general rule, it is helpful to compare the information that could be gleaned from any new susceptibility testing against our current benchmark "genetic test" for complex disorders, which is the family history. For most psychiatric disorders, the empiric risk to the first-degree relative of an affected individual is approximately 10%. Using this benchmark can help you work with clients to determine if the cost of the testing is worth the information that will be gained, and whether what will be gained is above and beyond what we already know about risk, based on family history.

When you evaluate any new genetic testing that may become available, it is important to consider the analytic validity (i.e., reliability and accuracy of the test), clinical validity (i.e., the strength of the evidence that the variant being tested plays a role in the condition in question—the test's sensitivity, specificity, positive predictive value, and negative predictive value), and clinical utility of the test (i.e., the risks and benefits of introducing the test in practice, including whether the test provides information that facilitates patient care) (Grosse & Khoury, 2006), as well as the ethical, legal, and social implications for the client, the client's family, and society (Mitchell et al., 2010). The complexity of this evaluation is one of the primary reasons why we recommend that mental health clinicians refer to, or consult with, genetics professionals prior to counseling about genetic testing. Several sources that provide more information about evaluating genetic testing are provided in the Appendix.

The Future of Genetic Susceptibility Testing for Psychiatric Illness

Over time, as researchers continue to identify the role and interaction of genes in psychiatric illness, new genetic testing may become available that the scientific community agrees has value for specific clients, and that is approved by professional and federal bodies as having clinical validity and utility. If and when such testing does become available, many practical and ethical issues will become even more urgently pertinent. Some of the issues include:

- *Meaning of the results*: For which disorder or class or disorders will the risk pertain? Will the results provide any information about age at onset, severity, or response to treatment?
- *Interventions*: What should health care clinicians tell at-risk individuals about risk-reduction strategies? Should high-risk individuals be treated differently on an individual or societal level, to protect them and to protect the best interests of society?
- *Education and counseling*: Who will help clients and their clinicians understand the scientific and statistical intricacies of susceptibility testing? Who will provide support and counseling prior to and after testing, and who will interpret the results?

- *Access*: To whom should testing be made available? Should everyone have access? Or should testing be available only those who are at increased risk based on family history? Should third-party payers cover the costs of susceptibility testing, and if so, what level of predictive ability should they require?
- *Privacy and confidentiality*: Who will have access to the test results, and what will third parties be allowed to do with the information?
- *Prenatal testing*: Should genetic susceptibility testing be offered prenatally? This is especially problematic because the test would not provide a yes or no answer, but rather an estimate of risk. The risk also may be for an adult-onset disorder, suggesting the likelihood of decades of disease-free life and the possibility of improved interventions and treatments before the predicted age at onset.

These are nontrivial issues that are far from being resolved. We present information about five ethical and legal concerns below: interpreting results over time, genetic testing of minors, the protection of genetic information, the potential psychological effects of the test information, and the impact on diagnosis and acceptance of diagnosis.

Interpreting Results over Time

For the foreseeable future we will not have a complete understanding of how the human genome affects health and disease. As our knowledge improves over time, it is likely that we will learn new and sometimes unexpected things about how particular genetic variants affect risk to particular disorders. In the context of genetic susceptibility testing for psychiatric disorders, we can expect to learn more about:

- How genes interact with each other, allowing the offering of multiple tests in a susceptibility panel
- How to integrate genetic data into other predictive information (e.g., data from magnetic resonance imaging [MRI] studies) to increase overall risk prediction

- How genes interact with specific environmental factors, allowing targeted interventions; and
- To what specific outcomes a gene or group of genes predisposes, including both psychiatric outcomes and risk for non-mental health disorders.

There will be some challenges to interpreting the data from susceptibility testing. How much risk is there? What is the risk for? How do other genetic and environmental components affect the risk? Laboratories and clinicians face important questions about our responsibilities for contacting and educating our clients who have had susceptibility testing as our increasing knowledge changes how we interpret their test results.

Genetic Testing of Minors

A challenging question related to the application of genetic testing is whether parents should be able to choose psychiatric susceptibility testing for their minor children. Let us assume that the purpose of susceptibility testing would be to determine which individuals are at highest risk in order to determine who might benefit from risk-reducing interventions. We can also assume that, based on the typical ages at onset for psychiatric illnesses, risk-reducing interventions will have the greatest impact if applied in childhood. This leads us to the conclusion that susceptibility testing for psychiatric illness may be appropriate to use in minors. Such testing in minors is typically approached with extreme caution in genetics, however. One reason for this caution is that minors cannot legally consent to such testing and thus the decision would be made by their guardians, effectively removing the minor's right not to know this potentially life-altering information. Another concern is that parents might alter their attitudes or behavior toward their tested "at-risk" and "not-at-risk" children in ways that could be harmful—for example, assuming that the at-risk child will become ill and thus limiting his or her life choices, or assuming that the not-at-risk child will not become ill and thus failing to notice emerging symptoms of mental illness and delaying seeking out appropriate help and intervention.

Protection of Genetic Information

There are disparate levels of protection across North America and Europe against release and sharing of genetic information. Although there have been few verified cases of genetic discrimination in the United States, some clients factor concerns about confidentiality and discrimination into decisions about whether to undergo genetic testing and what to do with the results (Klitzman, 2010); clinicians who have concerns about discrimination may refer to genetics less often (Lowstuter et al., 2008); and genetic counselors commonly discuss the potential for discrimination during counseling about genetic testing (Pfeffer et al., 2003). Genetic discrimination based on susceptibility for a common disorder, such as a psychiatric illness, is a newer area of concern and research. Because there is not yet meaningful genetic susceptibility testing available for most psychiatric disorders, confidentiality and discrimination concerns are not as pressing. It can be easily imagined, however, how concerning confidentiality and discrimination issues may become when susceptibility testing for psychiatric illnesses reaches a higher level of predictive value and becomes more widely available.

For example, consider a scenario where a military organization chose to test new recruits for predisposition to anxiety, depression, and posttraumatic stress disorder (PTSD). The military may have the recruits' best interests at heart—that is, the military might hope to shield at-risk individuals from intensely stressful combat experiences. Even so, several challenging questions remain. Would military commanders, health care clinicians, and soldiers understand the complex notion of susceptibility—a potential risk that may not ever manifest? Who would know the results of the susceptibility test? What would the military be permitted to do with the information? Would the test results be provided to the recruit, and if so, by whom, and with what sort of education and counseling?

In the Appendix we provide sources where clinicians can learn about the Genetic Information Nondiscrimination Act (GINA) of 2008. In the United States, GINA prohibits discrimination in health coverage and employment on the basis of genetic information. GINA, together with existing nondiscrimination provisions of the Health Insurance Portability and Accountability Act (HIPAA), generally prohibits health insurers or health plan administrators from requesting or requiring genetic information or using it for decisions regarding coverage, rates, or preexisting conditions. The law also prohibits most employers from using genetic information in decisions about hiring, firing, or promotion.

Impact of Genetic Information on Psychological Well-Being

Genetic susceptibility testing may allow some at-risk individuals to improve their psychological well-being in that they may be able to use the testing to increase their perceptions of control and make meaning of their risk for psychiatric illness. It is important not to discount the significance of a solely psychological benefit to genetic testing. On the other hand, the individuals who we expect will be most interested in susceptibility testing for psychiatric disorders—the ones with a family history of mental illness—may be the most likely to be harmed by the information. Individuals who are at risk for major psychiatric illnesses may be more sensitive to stressful life events and may be less likely to have strong support networks, e.g., a family history of psychosis has been suggested to reduce the coping capacity of relatives and reduce help-seeking behaviors and social support (St-Hilaire, Hill, & Docherty, 2007). It is conceivable that receiving a test result that indicates high risk for a particular psychiatric illness could be sufficiently stressful that it could actually act as a trigger for illness onset. Less dramatic but still worrisome is the concern that a test result indicating increased risk could induce substantial worry and monitoring of at-risk individuals by family members, especially given high perceived burden of these illnesses.

Impact on Diagnosis and Acceptance of Diagnosis

There are a number of ways in which the availability of a genetic susceptibility test for psychiatric illness could influence psychiatric diagnosis. There are many foreseeable benefits to the diagnostic process, including surveillance and early diagnoses of those known to be at increased risk, refining diagnostic categories such that they are more etiologically homogeneous, and using a particular genotype to predict illness course, long-term diagnosis, and the most effective treatment course. Genetic testing could be perceived as irrefutable personal information by some individuals, for whom the information may help foster an acceptance of their diagnoses.

There are also many concerns about the effects of genetic testing on diagnosis. Given that the diagnosis of psychiatric illness is based on clinical impression, clinicians could become vulnerable to a subconscious bias toward diagnosing illness in individuals shown to have increased genetic vulnerability when the individuals do not (and may never) meet the full diagnostic criteria. Further difficulty could arise if symptoms of psychiatric illness emerge but do not match the particular type of diagnosis that was expected based on the genetic test results. The fact that susceptibility alleles will likely confer risk to more than one specific psychiatric illness makes it likely that this will occur, but up-to-date information around these issues will be difficult to deliver to clients.

In addition, compared to many nonpsychiatric medical conditions, psychiatric diagnoses are less likely to be accepted by the individuals to whom they are applied. Individuals who wish—by way of obtaining a "negative" genetic test result—to gather data that support their belief that they do not have a psychiatric illness may inappropriately use susceptibility testing to discount their diagnosis. It is unlikely that any genetic test relevant to psychiatric illness could ever be correctly applied in this way, because the absence of a specific set of genetic vulnerability factors is unlikely to preclude the possibility of a psychiatric illness. Making these concepts clear to clients may be a challenge.

Although the idea of genetic susceptibility testing for psychiatric illness is exciting, it is important to remember that at least for the near future, the best way to determine the chance for an individual to develop a psychiatric illness will continue to be by evaluation of detailed psychiatric family history.

What You Can Say to Clients and Family Members about Genetic Susceptibility Testing

"Sometimes after learning about the role of genetics in the development of psychiatric illness, people wonder whether genetic testing is possible."

Raising this topic directly can sometimes be helpful as it allows you to segue into a discussion of the current limitations of genetic susceptibility testing for psychiatric illnesses, as outlined above. Without an explicit discussion of genetic testing and its limitations, at some time after the discussion many clients and family members logically arrive at the question of whether genetic testing is available. Internet searching may alert them to the availability of testing provided directly to the consumer, but they may then have little opportunity to discuss the implications and limitations of this testing (often not described in the marketing materials of the company advertising the test). This leaves the individual vulnerable to misunderstandings, wasted money, and negative psychological outcomes.

"Genetic testing is unlikely to ever be able to tell us with certainty who will and who will not develop psychiatric illness."

This is a critical concept for affected individuals and their family members to appreciate. It is frequently assumed that genetic testing can always provide definitive answers. For psychiatric illnesses any testing that becomes available is more likely to generate probabilistic information. Although some individuals find probabilistic information valuable, others will be interested only in definitive information.

"Any genetic testing that could be performed at the moment would not be very useful from a clinical perspective."

You could help people understand that the genetic variants that have been identified each seem to increase an individual's vulnerability to psychiatric illness by a very small amount. For example, while the general population risk for developing schizophrenia is in the region of 1%, an individual who has a genetic variant that confers vulnerability might have a risk of 2%. Though this is a doubling of risk, the absolute risk is still so low as to have no impact on services that might be available to that individual, or how you would clinically manage that person.

"If you are concerned, the best way to determine what the chance is for yourself/someone else in your family to develop psychiatric illness is to use a detailed psychiatric family history."

At present, the gold standard tool for estimating risk of psychiatric disorders is the family history. This can seem surprising, because technological approaches such as genetic testing are usually perceived as being more desirable and accurate than lower-tech approaches. You might find it useful confront this perception very concretely. This discussion also allows you to offer to talk about family history together or to make a referral to a genetic counselor.

Issues That Clients and Their Families May Raise

"Can I have a genetic test to see if I will develop a psychiatric illness like my family member did?"

It would be important to explore the motivation for this question to determine how to best meet the individual's needs. For example, a family member who is concerned that he or she is starting to experience the same symptoms as the affected relative may be better served by a psychiatric evaluation than by genetic testing. Assuming that the motivation is something other than the question of current symptoms, then the priority is to ensure that the individual is aware that, at present, no genetic tests have been deemed clinically valid or useful by the scientific community for determining susceptibility to psychiatric illness. The individual should understand that the genetic variants suspected to confer vulnerability do so to a very limited extent and that the testing will never be able to provide definitive information because of the roles of other genes and environment in illness causation. If the individual is interested in the most thorough assessment possible, inform him or her that this is possible, without genetic testing, by assessing a detailed psychiatric family history.

"I read a news article about a genetic test for psychiatric illness. I thought that [stress/drugs/other] caused my illness—how would a test about genes work?"

This question demonstrates great insight and is an indicator of this individual's desire for a broader discussion about the etiology of psychiatric illness. A good response to this kind of inquiry might involve appreciation of the question and an offer to talk about how the factor(s) the client identified may or may not have contributed to the development of his or her illness, and how genetics is involved. It could be helpful to ask your client to direct you to the news article so that you can review it together in the context of your discussion.

"I've had a genetic test, and it said that I am more likely to develop psychiatric illness, so now I'm really worried."

This is an appropriate scenario in which to direct the individual to a genetic counselor. Offer to sit down together and discuss what is known about the factors that contribute to the development of a psychiatric illness, and to talk about the test results in light of that knowledge. During this discussion, the critical factors to convey are your thoughts about the clinical validity and utility of the test and what the results mean in terms of risk. A referral to a genetic counselor would provide the client with a more comprehensive evaluation of the test and the results.

Our Experience

Case Example

Janet and Tony had two children. Stephanie, age 15, had just experienced her first episode of psychosis. Her brother Steven, age 12, was healthy. Janet and Tony were familiar with psychiatric illness because both had affected siblings, and they recognized it quickly in their daughter. They found their experience with Stephanie's illness very difficult and indicated that it took its toll on the whole family. Based on their family history, they attributed their daughter's illness to genetics. They came to see me wanting to know if predictive testing was available that would tell them whether their son would develop the same condition. Janet and Tony felt that if the predictive test were positive, they would "pull out all the stops" and try all the preventive therapies that they could find.

My (JA) approach with the couple was to give them an opportunity to express their feelings about their daughter's illness and its impact on them as individuals and as a family, particularly in light of their family histories. I then discussed the current state of knowledge about the etiology of schizophrenia. During the course of this discussion, the couple realized for themselves that if environmental factors were important in illness development (and this made sense to them, based on their own siblings' circumstances around the time the illness emerged, and in terms of what Stephanie had been through), then genetic testing would not be able to tell them for sure whether their son would develop the illness. They immediately said that they would not be interested in testing if the results were not yes or no. They also realized that many of the strategies they were employing with Stephanie to keep her well (including sleep, good nutrition, exercise, learning to reduce and manage stress) could also be used with Steven in an effort to protect his mental health. They also raised concerns about the impact of his sister's illness on Steven, including his own anxiety and fear about his mental health and possible feelings of shame and guilt. We talked about some strategies for maintaining good communication around these difficult issues. Janet and Tony realized that their desire for testing was based on fear, which was exacerbated by the difficulty of distinguishing normal adolescent behavior from emerging psychotic symptoms. They were able to appreciate the potential for a negative impact of genetic testing on their son's well-being, given the current status of this kind of testing. Janet and Tony concluded the session noting that they no longer wanted testing for their son, and that they felt prepared to do what they could to make sure he felt supported. Although they would have preferred a sure-fire strategy by which psychiatric illness could be prevented for him, they could accept that this was not possible and were ready to work toward trying to minimize his risk.

CHAPTER TWELVE

How to Talk About Genetic Testing to Inform Medication Strategy

Personalized Medicine

Although the use of genetic testing to inform medication strategy is an area of research that often gets less attention than genetic susceptibility testing, it is perhaps more likely to have significant therapeutic impact in the near future. It involves looking for genetic variations that influence how an individual responds to a particular psychiatric medication. This area of research is known as psychopharmacogenetics or psychopharmacogenomics; the former is used to describe the investigation of the influence of individual genetic variations on an individual's response to a psychiatric medication, and the latter relates to investigating the influence of variations across the whole genome on an individual's response to a psychiatric medication. In practice, the terms are often used interchangeably.

When two individuals with the same condition are prescribed the same medication in the same dose in order to treat the same symptoms, the individuals may nevertheless differ in their response to the drug. One individual may experience relief of the targeted symptoms while suffering no undesired side effects, whereas the other may have no relief of targeted symptoms or may experience undesired side effects. For the latter individual, traditionally the next steps may be dosage modifications, tapering off one medication and starting a dosage titration with a new medication, and so on, until the clinician identifies an effective medication or combination of medications. This unpredictability of treatment response can be frustrating for both client and clinician. The mechanism by which two individuals can have very different responses to the same dose of the same medication is thought to be based, at least in part, on differences between the two individuals in genes that encode the proteins that play important roles in allowing the body to process medications. The ultimate goal of psychopharmacogenomic research is to be able to tailor medication selections to each individual based on his or her genetic information, thus bypassing the need for the burdensome and distressing trial-and-error process of medication selection and dosing. Such endeavors have been labeled *personalized medicine.*

In the United States, pharmacogenetic testing is increasingly being incorporated into clinical practice in the treatment of a number of conditions, including certain kinds of cancer and cardiovascular disease. The FDA-approved package labeling for warfarin, one of the most frequently prescribed drugs to prevent blood clots, heart attack, and stroke, includes a reference to a genetic variation that influences how clients respond to the drug. Although pharmacogenetic testing for response to psychiatric medications is not as advanced as some other areas, it holds significant promise. Researchers are currently attempting to identify genetic variations that influence:

• Weight gain in response to atypical antipsychotics
• Tardive dyskinesia in response to typical antipsychotics
• Agranulocytosis in response to clozapine treatment
• Response to lithium, SSRIs, and other psychotropic medications

At present, there are not enough data to establish the clinical validity and utility of pharmacogenetic tests (for example, see EGAPP working group, 2007). These data are required before such tests become part of the standard of psychiatric care in North America. It is likely that as data accumulate, some pharmacogenetic tests will be shown to be effective in determining a strategy for pharmacological treatment. It is already possible for mental health professionals to order certain pharmacogenetic tests from online companies and commercial laboratories. At present the available tests are limited primarily to those that provide insight into whether an individual is a "fast" or "slow" metabolizer of certain classes of psychiatric medications. Although there are insufficient data to support their utility for all clients at this point in the research, pharmagogenetic testing may offer benefit for some groups of clients—for example, clients whose symptoms persist despite trials of different medications at different doses (see the Appendix for information about options for this kind of pharmacogenetic testing).

In the same way that genetic vulnerability to psychiatric illness may be shared among biological relatives, the genetic factors that influence the way in which individuals respond to different psychiatric medications may also be shared by these individuals. This phenomenon can be clearly observed in clinical practice. Studies have shown that response to lithium (administered as a treatment for bipolar disorder, among other conditions) has a familial component, in that if one family member has responded well to lithium there is a good chance that other family members with the same diagnosis will respond well too (Grof et al., 1994). Conversely, if one affected individual does not respond well to lithium, there is a greater chance that relatives with the same illness will react to this drug in a similar way.

What You Can Say to Clients and Family Members about Psychopharmacogenomics

"Genes tell our bodies how to make proteins, including the proteins that are responsible for helping us to break down and make use of medications. Genetic differences mean that some

people will respond well to a medication and others will respond less well."

This kind of explanation will be comprehensible to many clients, particularly if it is introduced subsequent to a discussion of illness etiology. It can be used to introduce explanations of why different medications work for different individuals, why a medication may not be working for a particular client or may have unacceptable side effects, or why a medication that works well for a relative of your client might be a good option to prescribe for the client, too.

"In the same way that genes that increase the chance for psychiatric illness can be passed through families, the genes that help us break down and use medications can also be passed through families. So if we know that you respond well to lithium, there is a good chance that your affected family members will also respond well to lithium."

Once a client has a basic understanding of how genetic factors can contribute to the development of a psychiatric illness, the clinician can frame the concept behind psychopharmacogenomics in a similar way. This can be helpful when discussing medication strategy for someone newly diagnosed with a disorder, or to justify a trial with the same medication used by a relative in a client who had suboptimal experiences with other medications.

Issues That Clients and Their Families May Raise

"My sister had some kind of test to work out what dose to use for her depression medication—do I need the same thing?"

Clinicians should explain that there is growing evidence for the use of genes to help predict the proper drug dose, but that we still need more information before it is clear when pharmacogenetic tests should be applied and how clinicians should use the results. The client certainly does not *need* to have the same test, and if he or she is stable on medication, the test may offer little or no benefit.

"I saw a blog about genetic testing; it said that the test would make it so that I could find a medicine that doesn't have any of the really annoying side effects that I have now. Can I have it?"

It is useful for the clinician to explain the concept behind pharmacogenetic testing and help the client understand the potential for pharmacogenetic testing to reduce side effects. The clinician should explain that we do not yet have all of the information we need to really understand how to best use the technology, though. The discussion that ensues would depend on the client's psychiatric and medication history; it may be that consideration of a different dosing plan or a different medication may be the most appealing next step. In some cases the client and clinician may decide that the pharmacogenetic testing is a good step to inform the client's care. In other cases, it may not be appropriate and the current regimen, flawed though it may be, is the best available.

Our Experience

We have had numerous experiences in which mental health clinicians have consulted us about pharmacogenetic testing. They often ask our opinion about whether pharmacogenetic testing is ready for clinical use. As we describe above, sufficient data are not yet available to provide a clear answer about if and when pharmacogenetic testing should be integrated into clinical care. Even if the data made the appropriate use of such testing more clear-cut, the question of whether the test is worth the money would remain. We encourage you to engage clients in discussions about cost in a similar way that we engage our own clients in discussions about the cost of many different types of genetic testing. This conversation requires that you help the client understand the potential benefits and limitations of the pharmacogenetic testing, and then help the client weigh those against the benefits and limitations of the current approach to medication choice and dosing. Finally, if there are reasonable benefits to an approach informed by pharmacogenetic testing, you can help the client determine if those benefits are worth the (literal) cost of the test. Through these discussions, you should try to ensure that clients understand what they will get from the testing so that they are informed consumers.

CHAPTER THIRTEEN

Looking Forward

How You and Your Client Might Benefit from a More Complete Understanding of Etiology

New genetic approaches and the application of new technologies to our current approaches will allow researchers to continue to elucidate the genetic contributions to psychiatric illness. In turn, a better understanding of the genetic etiology will facilitate studies to identify the environmental components and will improve our understanding of the pathophysiology of psychiatric illness. You will be able to use the core concepts in this book as the basis upon which to integrate the improved understanding of etiology into your practice.

Risk Assessment

As described throughout this book, our current ability to provide clients and family members with individualized risk assessment is limited by the complex and heterogeneous nature of psychiatric diagnoses and by the relative paucity of empiric risk data that address the diversity found in psychiatric family histories. In the relatively near term, we expect that clinicians and clients may benefit from a more diverse range of empiric risk data. For example, consider a relative who has one affected sibling and one affected cousin; currently, empiric risks for this particular combination of affected relatives do not exist. Improved empiric risk data will allow us to better estimate the risk, given the family history.

In time, genotyping of affected individuals may allow improved characterization of the illness in the family (e.g., a particular subtype of bipolar I disorder). Genotyping at-risk individuals may result in an estimation of risk for the illness that can be interpreted in light of the family history, thus improving our ability to provide accurate risk assessment. It may be possible to tailor risk assessment even further if researchers are able to identify environmental risk factors that can be accurately measured in at-risk individuals. For example, a confirmed exposure to a particular virus in the at-risk individual might add an additional, quantifiable amount of risk.

It is also possible that researchers will identify and describe traits that will be useful in identifying those relatives who have increased familial risk for particular psychiatric disorders. The idea is that some traits are associated with some subset of the susceptibility factors that lead to the psychiatric disorder; that is, these traits represent an intermediary effect between particular susceptibility gene(s) and the full complement of illness features. Thus, it is reasonable to think that if an individual with a particular disorder—for example, schizophrenia—has a particular trait—for example, a brain alteration leading to a specific MRI finding—his or her relatives who have the same MRI finding might be at higher risk than relatives who do not have the MRI finding.

Even with these advances, however, we expect that the family history will continue to be very important to help identify those who would benefit from genetic testing and to help interpret the results from genetic tests. It is likely that the advent of genetic susceptibility testing will make it more important, not less, for clinicians to collect and evaluate family history.

Risk Reduction

As described in Chapter 12, genetic information will increasingly be used to identify who is most likely to benefit from particular therapies (pharmacogenetics). There is also real hope that an improved understanding of disorder pathophysiology will lead to preventive efforts for at-risk individuals. A better understanding of gene–environment interactions yields the potential to identify possible modification strategies in relation to environmental risk. These include efforts that would, through parent interventions with children and/or therapy with children and adults, counter an individual's genetically mediated traits and behaviors by changing the social environment and modifying how others respond to the individual. Other modifications might be chemically-based (e.g., offering specific nutritional supplements or medications based on a client's genetic information), or lifestyle- or aversion-based (e.g., receiving advice about factors to seek out or avoid based on genetic information and medical history). We also expect that, in the longer term, data from studies evaluating risk modification efforts will provide concrete evidence about the effectiveness of risk-reduction efforts, some of which may be feasible to implement on a population level to reduce the overall incidence of psychiatric illness.

Improvements in Diagnosis and Management

Longer term, it is not unreasonable to expect that the current psychiatric diagnostic system will be replaced with one that is based on both the results of laboratory tests (including genetic tests) and clinical symptoms. Clinicians will be better able to predict clinical course and outcomes, including who is likely to benefit from pharmacological approaches, psychotherapeutic approaches, or a combined approach. In addition, we can anticipate rational drug development—that is, new therapeutics will be developed based on novel biological targets identified as important by genetic research.

Genetic Susceptibility Testing

Once researchers have a much better understanding of the factors that confer genetic vulnerability and how they interact, we expect that genetic testing may achieve acceptable clinical utility and become readily available through reputable commercial and academic laboratories. Susceptibility genetic testing should allow much-improved prediction of who is at the most and the least risk for psychiatric illness—though the complexity of the illness (including the contribution of life experience and environment) makes it very unlikely that we will ever achieve definitive "yes or no" answers from such testing.

Gene Therapy

Though gene therapy gets a great deal of public attention, there are many caveats with regard to its application as a possible "cure" of psychiatric illness. Gene therapy relies on delivering a functional "replacement" copy of a gene into a cell in which the existing gene has a variation that has a negative impact. There are many issues with implementing gene therapy for psychiatric illness. Such therapy would likely have to be able to target multiple susceptibility genes to have a significant effect, and would have to be applied to the affected organ—the brain—which is quite difficult to access. Further, with regard to the prevention of psychiatric illness, gene therapy is not without risk and thus it would be difficult to weigh the risk associated with its use in at-risk individuals who may never develop illness. Finally, and perhaps most importantly, none of the gene variants that increases risk to psychiatric disorders is "the" gene for psychiatric illness. It is naïve to think that the genes that increase vulnerability do not also play other, potentially important roles in our overall mental and physical well-being, and perhaps the adaptation of our species. Modifying genes that exert important effects on behavior and our response to the environment is a risky undertaking.

Conclusion

We would like to leave you with an appreciation of the incredible variety and flexibility that genetic variability provides in humankind. Such variation likely contributes to our species' tremendous capacity for innovation and creativity. The same kinds of variation sometimes result in maladaptive responses to the environment, including issues with mood and cognition. Because human variation is random, "positive" variation is not possible without "negative" variation, and in fact we are likely to find that the same variant leads to adaptive or maladaptive responses depending on the individual's overall genotype and environmental context. Overall, our genetic variation has allowed our species to adapt remarkably well to our changing environment.

We hope that this book has provided you with a greater appreciation of the complex etiology of psychiatric disorders; an increased ability to evaluate and communicate familial risk; an appreciation of why and how one might integrate this information into mental health practice; the ability to begin or enhance communication with genetics colleagues; and a better understanding of the benefits that education and counseling about etiology and family risk can have for clients and their family members.

Appendix

Further Reading and Resources

General Genetics

Websites

Learn.Genetics website, Genetic Science Learning Center, University of Utah

http://learn.genetics.utah.edu/

National Coalition for Health Professional Education in Genetics website

http://www.nchpeg.org

American College of Medical Genetics: Genetics for Providers

http://www.acmg.net/AM/Template.cfm?Section=CME_Activities&Template=/CM/HTMLDisplay.cfm&ContentID=3106

National Human Genome Research Institute: Resources for Health Professionals

http://www.genome.gov/HealthProfessionals/

National Human Genome Research Institute: Basic Genetics

http://www.genome.gov/Education/

My Family Health Portrait (family history tool)

https://familyhistory.hhs.gov/

National Society of Genetic Counselors: Your Family History, Your Future (family history tool)

http://www.nsgc.org/consumer/familytree/index.cfm

Genetic Alliance: Family Health History toolkit
  http://www.geneticalliance.org/fhh
Genetic Alliance: WikiGenetics
  http://www.geneticalliance.org/wiki

Articles

Attia, J., Ioannidis, J.P., Thakkinstian, A., McEvoy, M., Scott, R.J., Minelli, C., et al. (2009). How to use an article about genetic association: A: Background concepts. *Journal of the American Medical Association, 301*(1), 74-81.

Attia, J., Ioannidis, J.P., Thakkinstian, A., McEvoy, M., Scott, R.J., Minelli, C., et al. (2009). How to use an article about genetic association: B: Are the results of the study valid? *Journal of the American Medical Association, 301*(2), 191-197.

Attia, J., Ioannidis, J.P., Thakkinstian, A., McEvoy, M., Scott, R.J., Minelli, C., et al. (2009). How to use an article about genetic association? *Journal of the American Medical Association, 301*(3), 304-308.

Psychiatric Genetics

Websites

RC Psych CDP Online: Genetics for Psychiatrists (Smith, D., Craddock, N., O'Donovan, M., & Owen, M.): www.psychiatrycpd.co.uk/learningmodules/geneticsforpsychiatrists.aspx

Exploring Autism: A Look at the Genetics of Autism, Frequently Asked Questions: http://www.exploringautism.org/faq.htm

National Institute of Mental Health: Science News about Genetics: http://www.nimh.nih.gov/science-news/science-news-about-genetics.shtml

Books

Baker, C. (2004). *Behavioral genetics: An introduction to how genes and environments interact through development to shape differences in mood, personality, and intelligence.* Washington, DC: American Association for the Advancement of Science.

Smoller, J., Shiedley, B., & Tsuang, M. (Eds.). (2008). *Psychiatric genetics: Applications in clinical practice.* Washington DC: American Psychiatric Association.

Genetic Counseling

Website

National Society of Genetic Counselors
http://www.nsgc.org

Books

Baker, D., Scheuette, J., & Uhlmann, W. (Eds.). (2009). *A guide to genetic counseling* (2nd ed.). New York: Wiley.

Weil, J. (2000). *Psychosocial genetic counseling.* New York: Oxford University Press.

Peay, H.L., & Hadley, D. (2009). Genetic counseling. In B.J. Sadock, V.A. Sadock, & P. Ruiz (Eds.), *Kaplan and Sadock's comprehensive textbook of psychiatry* (9th ed.). New York: Lippincott, Williams & Wilkins.

Risk Assessment and Counseling

Website

NSGC Healthcare Provider Site, Psychiatric Genetics Special Interest Group page http://www.nsgc.org/providers/

Articles

Austin, J.C., Palmer, C., Rosen-Sheidley, B., McCarthy-Veach, P., Gettig, B., & Peay, H.L. (2007). Psychiatric disorders in clinical genetics II: Individualizing recurrence risks. *Journal of Genetic Counseling*, *17*(1), 18–29.

Austin, J.C,. & Peay, H.L. (2006). Applications and limitations of empiric data in provision of recurrence risks for schizophrenia: A practical review for healthcare professionals providing clinical psychiatric genetics consultations. *Clinical Genetics*, *70*(3), 177–187.

Genetic Susceptibility Testing

Websites

Schizophrenia Forum
   http://www.Schizophreniaforum.org
ACCE Model Process for Evaluating Genetic Tests
   http://www.cdc.gov/genomics/gtesting/ACCE/index.htm

Article

Burke, W. (2009). Clinical validity and clinical utility of genetic tests. *Current Protocol in Human Genetics*, Jan; Chapter 9:Unit 9.15.

Pharmacogenetic Testing

Websites

Pharmacy.ca Personalized Medicine
   http://pharmacy.ca
Cincinnati Children's Pharmacogenetic Testing Service
   http://www.cincinnatichildrens.org/svc/alpha/g/gps/drugs.htm

Mayo Clinic Testing

    http://www.mayoclinic.org/depression/cytochrome.html

Genelex Testing

    http://www.healthanddna.com

Book

Mrazek, D. (2010). *Psychiatric pharmacogenomics*. New York: Oxford University Press.

Referral Resources

National Society of Genetic Counselors

    http://www.nsgc.org

Canadian Association of Genetic Counselors

    http://www.cagc-accg.ca

American Society of Human Genetics

    http://www.ashg.org

Resources for Specific Clients

Pregnant Clients

Supporting Families with Parental Mental Illness or Problematic Substance Use: Ulysses Agreement

    http://www.parentalmentalillness.org/Ulysses_tip_sheet.html

Organization of Teratology Information Specialists: www.otispregnancy.org

Parents of At-Risk Children

International Early Psychosis Association

    www.iepa.org.au

Websites of early psychosis intervention programs:

http://www.psychosissucks.ca (British Columbia, Canada)

http://oyh.org.au/ (Australia)

http://www.eppic.org.au/ (Australia)

http://www.iris-initiative.org.uk (UK)

Centre for Addiction and Mental Health, University of Toronto: When a Parent Has Bipolar Disorder . . . What Kids Want to Know

http://www.camh.net/about_addiction_mental_health/mental_health_information/when_parent_bipolar.html

Centre for Addiction and Mental Health, University of Toronto: When a Parent Has Psychosis . . . What Kids Want to Know

http://www.camh.net/About_Addiction_Mental_Health/Mental_Health_Information/when_parent_psychosis.html

Centre for Addiction and Mental Health, University of Toronto: When a Parent Has Depression . . . What Kids Want to Know

http://www.camh.net/About_Addiction_Mental_Health/Mental_Health_Information/when_parent_depressed.html

Goodman, S., & Gotlib, I. (Ed.). (2002). *Children of depressed parents: Mechanisms of risk and implications for treatment.* Washington, DC: American Psychological Association.

Birchwood, M., Fowler, D., & Jackson, C. (Eds.) (2000). Early intervention in psychosis: A guide to concepts, evidence and interventions. West Sussex, UK: Wiley.

Parents of Affected Children

Child and Adolescent Bipolar Foundation

http://www.bpkids.org

Prevalence of autism spectrum disorders: http://www.cdc.gov/mmwr/preview/mmwrhtml/ss5810a1.htm

Rapoport, J. (Ed.). (2000). *Childhood onset of "adult" psychopathology: Clinical and research advances.* Washington, DC: American Psychiatric Association.

Schaefer, B., & Mendelsohn, N. (2008). Genetics evaluation for the etiologic diagnosis of autism spectrum disorders. *Genetics in Medicine*, *10*(1), 4-12.

Unaffected Family Members

Bipolar Significant Others: http://www.bpso.org/
Centre for Addiction and Mental Health, University of Toronto: Schizophrenia—Help for Partners and Family
    http://www.camh.net/About_Addiction_Mental_Health/Mental_
    Health_Information/schizophrenia_partfam.html

Support/Advocacy Organizations and Mental Illness Information

National Alliance for the Mentally Ill (NAMI)
    http://www.nami.org
Depression and Bipolar Support Association
    http://www.dpsalliance.org
NARSAD: The Brain and Behavior Research Fund
    http://www.narsad.org
Schizophrenia Society of Canada
    http://www.schizophrenia.ca/
Rethink (UK)
    http://www.rethink.org/
Mood Disorders Association Canada
    http://www.mooddisorderscanada.ca/
Mental Health America
    http://www.nmha.org/
Canadian Mental Health Association
    www.cmha.ca
World Federation for Mental Health
    http://www.wfmh.org/

References

Alaban, F. (1999). Primer in folic acid: Folates and neuropsychiatry. *Nutrition, 15*(7/8), 595-99.

Alloy, L. B., Abramson, L. Y., Urosevic, S., Walshaw, P. D., Nusslock, R., & Neeren, A. M. (2005). The psychosocial context of bipolar disorder: Environmental, cognitive, and developmental risk factors. *Clinical Psychology Review, 25*(8), 1043-75.

American Academy of Pediatrics Committee on Drugs. (2000). Use of psychoactive medication during pregnancy and possible effects on the fetus and newborn. *Pediatrics, 105*(4), 880-87.

American Academy of Pediatrics Committee on Genetics. (1999). Folic acid for the prevention of neural tube defects. *Pediatrics, 104*(2), 325-27.

Amminger, G. P., Schafer, M. R., Papageorgiou, K., Klier, C. M., Cotton, S. M., Harrigan, S. M., Mackinnon, A., McGorry, P. D., & Berger, G. E. (2010). Long-chain omega-3 fatty acids for indicated prevention of psychotic disorders: A randomized placebo controlled trial. *American Journal of Psychiatry, 67*(2), 146-54.

Andorno, R. (2004). The right not to know: An autonomy based approach. *Journal of Medical Ethics, 30*, 435-40.

Angermeyer, M. C., Schulze, B., & Dietrich, S. (2003). Courtesy stigma—a focus group study of relatives of schizophrenia patients. *Social Psychiatry and Psychiatric Epidemiology, 38*(10), 593-602.

Austin, J. C., Smith, G. N., & Honer, W. G. (2006). The genomic era and perceptions of psychotic disorders: Genetic risk estimation, associations with reproductive decisions, and views about predictive testing. *American Journal of Medical Genetics, 141B,* 926-28.

Austin, J. C., & Peay, H. L. (2006). Applications and limitations of empiric data in provision of recurrence risks for schizophrenia: A practical review for healthcare professionals providing clinical psychiatric genetics consultations. *Clinical Genetics, 70*(3), 177-87.

Beardslee, W.R., Gladstone, T.R., Wright, E.J., Cooper, A.B. (2003). A family-based approach to the prevention of depressive symptoms in children at risk: Evidence of parental and child change. *Pediatrics, 112*(2), e119-31.

Bennett, R. L., French, K. S., Resta, R. G., & Doyle, D. L. (2008). Standardized human pedigree nomenclature: Update and assessment of the recommendations of the National Society of Genetic Counselors. *Journal of Genetic Counseling, 17,* 424-33.

Berrettini, W. H. (2000). Are schizophrenic and bipolar disorders related? A review of family and molecular studies. *Biological Psychiatry, 48*(6), 531-38.

Birmaher, B., Axelson, D., Goldstein, B., Monk, K., Kalas, C., Obreja, M., Hickey, M. B., Iyengar, S., Brent, D., Shamseddeen, W., Diler, R., & Kupfer, D. (2010). Psychiatric disorders in preschool offspring of parents with bipolar disorder: The Pittsburgh offspring study. *American Journal of Psychiatry, 167*(3), 321-30.

Bolton, P. F., Pickles, A., Murphy, M., & Rutter, M. (1998). Autism, affective and other psychiatric disorders: Patterns of familial aggregation. *Psychol Med, 28*(2), 385-95.

Bolton, P., MacDonald, H., Pickles, A., Rios, P., Goode, S., Crowson, M., et al. (1994). A case-control family history study of autism. *Journal of Child Psychology and Psychiatry, 35,* 877-900.

Brown, A. S., Derkits, E. J. (2010). Prenatal infection and schizophrenia: A review of epidemiological and translational studies. *American Journal of Psychiatry, 167*(3), 261-80.

Cannon, M., Jones, P. B., & Murray, R. M. (2002). Obstetric complications and schizophrenia: Historical and meta-analytic review. *American Journal of Psychiatry, 159*(7), 1080–92.

Cardno, A. G., Marshall, E. J., Coid, B., Macdonald, A. M., Ribchester, T. R., Davies, N. J., Venturi, P., Jones, L. A., Lewis, S. W., Sham, P. C., Gottesman, I. I., Farmer, A. E., McGuffin, P., Reveley, A. M., & Murray, R. M. (1999). Heritability estimates for psychotic disorders: The Maudsley twin psychosis series. *Archives of General Psychiatry, 56*(2), 162–68.

Cardon, L. R., & Bell, J. I. (2001). Association study designs for complex diseases. *Nature Reviews Genetics, 2*, 91–99.

Caspi, A., Moffit, T. E., Cannon, M., McClay, J., Murray, R., Harrington, H., Taylor, A., Arseneault, L., Williams, B., Braithwaite, A., Poulton, R., & Craig, I. W. (2005). Moderation of the effect of adolescent-onset cannabis use on adult psychosis by a functional polymorphism in the catechol-o-methyltransferase gene: Longitudinal evidence of a gene X environment interaction. *Biological Psychiatry, 57*, 1117–27.

Chapman, T. F., Mannuzza, S., Klein, D. F., & Fyer, A. J. (1994). Effects of informant mental disorder on psychiatric family history data. *American Journal of Psychiatry, 151*(4), 574–79.

Cichon, S., Craddock, N., Daly, M., Faraone, S. V., Gejman, P. V., Kelsoe, J., Lehner, T., Levinson, D. F., Moran, A., Sklar, P., & Sullivan, P. F. (Psychiatric GWAS Consortium Coordinating Committee). (2009). Genomewide association studies: History, rationale, and prospects for psychiatric disorders. *American Journal of Psychiatry, 166*(5), 540–56.

Cooper, B. (2001). Nature, nurture and mental disorder: Old concepts in the new millennium. *British Journal of Psychiatry, 40*, s91–101.

Coors, M. (2005). Genes in families: Attitudes toward genetic testing for schizophrenia. *Schizophrenia Research, 72*, 271–73.

Corcoran, C., Malaspina, D., Hercher, L. (2005). Prodromal interventions for schizophrenia vulnerability: The risks of being at risk. *Schizophrenia Research, 2005*(73), 175–84.

Corvin, A., Craddock, N., Sullivan, P.F. (2009). Genome wide association studies: A primer. *Psychological Medicine, 9,* 1-15.

Craddock, N., O'Donovan, M. C., Owen, M. J. (2006). Genes for schizophrenia and bipolar disorder: Implications for psychiatric nosology. *Schizophrenia Bulletin, 32*(1), 9-16.

Craig, E. A. (2004). Parenting programs for women with mental illness who have young children: A review. *Australia and New Zealand Journal of Psychiatry, 38*(11-12), 923-28.

Dalman, C., Allebeck, P., Gunnell, D., Harrison, G., Kristensson, K., Lewis, G., Lofving, S., Rasmussen, F., Wicks, S., & Karlsson, H. (2008). Infections in the CNS during childhood and the risk of subsequent psychotic illness: A cohort study of more than one million Swedish subjects. *American Journal of Psychiatry, 165*(1), 59-65.

Degenhardt, L., Hall, W., & Lynskey, M. (2003). Testing hypotheses about the relationship between cannabis use and psychosis. *Drug and Alcohol Dependence, 71,* 37-48.

DeStefano, F., & Thompson, W. W. (2004). MMR vaccine and autism: An update on the scientific evidence. *Expert Review of Vaccines, 3*(1), 19-22.

EGAPP Working Group (2007). Recommendations from the EGAPP working group: Testing for cytochrome P450 polymorphisms in adults with nonpsychotic depression treated with selective serotonin reuptake inhibitors. *Genetics in Medicine, 9*(12), 819-25.

Evers-Kiebooms, G., & Decruyenaere M. (1998). Predictive testing for Huntington's disease: A challenge for persons at risk and for professionals. *Patient Education and Counseling, 35,* 15-26.

Farooq, S., Large, M., Nielssen, O., & Waheed, W. (2009). The relationship between the duration of untreated psychosis and outcome in low-and-middle income countries: A systematic review and meta analysis. *Schizophrenia Research, 109*(1-3), 15-23.

Finn, C. T., & Smoller, J. W. (2006). Genetic counseling in psychiatry. *Harvard Review of Psychiatry, 14,* 109-21.

Finn, C. T., Wilcox, M. A., Korf, B. R., Blacker, D., Racette, S. R., Sklar,

P., & Smoller, J. W. (2005). Psychiatric genetics: A survey of psychiatrists' knowledge, opinions and practice patterns. *Journal of Clinical Psychiatry*, *66*(7), 821–30.

Friedman, J. M. & Polifka, J. E. (1998). *The effects of neurologic and psychiatric drugs on the fetus and nursing infant.* Baltimore: Johns Hopkins University Press.

Gorczynski, P., & Faulkner, G. (2010). Exercise therapy for schizophrenia. *Cochrane Database of Systematic Reviews*, *12*(5), CD004412.

Gottesman, I. I., Laursen, T. M., Bertelsen, A., & Mortensen, P. B. (2010). Severe mental disorders in offspring with 2 psychiatrically ill parents. *Archives of General Psychiatry*, *67*(3), 252–57.

Grelotti, D. J., Kanayama, G., & Pope, H. G. (2010). Remission of persistent methamphetamine-induced psychosis after electroconvulsive therapy: Presentation of a case and review of the literature. *American Journal of Psychiatry*, *167*(1), 17–23.

Grof, P., Alda., M., Grof, E., Zvolsky, P., & Walsh, M. (1994). Lithium response and genetics of affective disorders. *Journal of Affective Disorders*, *32*, 85–95.

Grosse, S. D., & Khoury, M. J. (2006). What is the clinical utility of genetic testing? *Genetics in Medicine*, *8*(7), 448–50.

Gusella, J. F., Wexler, N. S., Conneally, P. M., Nylor, S. L., Anderson, M. A., Tanzi, R. E., Watckins, P. C., Ottina, K., et al. (1983). A polymorphic DNA marker genetically linked to Huntington's disease. *Nature*, *306*, 234–38.

Haukka, J., Suvisaari, J., & Lonnqvist, J. (2003). Fertility of patients with schizophrenia, their siblings and the general population: A cohort study from 1950 to 1959 in Finland. *American Journal of Psychiatry*, *160*, 460–63.

Hicks, B. M., DiRago, A. C., Iacono, W. G., & McGue, M. (2009). Gene-environment interplay in internalizing disorders: Consistent findings across six environmental risk factors. *Journal of Child Psychology and Psychiatry, 50*(10), 1309–17.

Hoek, H. W., Brown, A. S., & Susser, E. (1998). The Dutch famine and schizophrenia spectrum disorders. *Social Psychiatry and Psychiatric Epidemiology, 33,* 373–79.

Hooley, J. M. (2007). Expressed emotion and relapse of psychopathology. *Annual Review of Clinical Psychology, 3,* 329–52.

Howard, L. (2004). Postnatal depression. *Clinical Evidence, 12,* 2000–15.

Hunter, M. J., Hippman, C., Honer, W. G., & Austin, J. C. (2010). Genetic counseling for schizophrenia: A review of referrals to a provincial medical genetics program from 1968 to 2007. *American Journal of Medical Genetics, 152A,* 147–52.

Hutchinson, G., & Haasen, C. (2004). Migration and schizophrenia: The challenges for European psychiatry and implications for the future. *Social Psychiatry and Psychiatric Epidemiology, 39,* 350–57.

Ingraham, L. J., & Kety, S. S. (2000). Adoption studies of schizophrenia. *American Journal of Medical Genetics, 97C,* 18–22.

Iwamoto, K., Kato, T. (2009). Epigenetic profiling in schizophrenia and major mental disorders. *Neuropsychobiology, 60*(1), 5–11.

Jones, I., Scourfield, J., McCandless, F., & Craddock, N. (2002). Attitudes towards future testing for bipolar disorder susceptibility genes: A preliminary investigation. *Journal of Affective Disorders, 71*(1–3), 189–93.

Jorge, R., & Robinson, R. G. (2003). Mood disorder following traumatic brain injury. *International Review of Psychiatry, 15*(4), 317–27.

Joseph, M. F., Youngstrom, E. A., & Soares, J. C. (2009). Antidepressant-coincident mania in children and adolescents treated with selective serotonin reuptake inhibitors. *Future Neurology, 4*(1), 87–102.

Kendler, K. S., & Gardner, C. O. (1997). The risk for psychiatric disorders in relatives of schizophrenic and control probands: A comparison of three independent studies. *Psychological Medicine, 27*(2), 411–19.

Kendler, K. S., & Prescott, C. A. (1999). A population-based twin study of lifetime major depression in men and women. *Archives of General Psychiatry, 56*(1), 39-44.

Kim, E. (2008). Does traumatic brain injury predispose individuals to develop schizophrenia? *Current Opinion in Psychiatry, 21*(3), 286-89.

Klitzman, R. (2010). Views of discrimination among individuals confronting genetic disease. *Journal of Genetic Counseling, 19*(1), 68-83.

Kreek, M. J., Nielsen, D. A., Butelman, E. R., & LaForge, K. S. (2005). Genetic influences on impulsivity, risk taking, stress responsivity and vulnerability to drug abuse and addiction. *Nature Neuroscience, 8*, 1450-57.

Laursen, T. M., Labouriau, R., Licht, R. W., Bertelsen, A., Munk-Olsen, T., & Mortensen, P. B. (2005). Family history of psychiatric illness as a risk factor for schizoaffective disorder. *Archives of General Psychiatry, 62*, 841-48.

Laursen, T. M., Munk-Olsen, T., Nordentoft, M., & Mortensen, & P. B. (2007). A comparison of selected risk factors for unipolar depressive disorder, bipolar disorder, schizoaffective disorder, and schizophrenia from a Danish population-based cohort. *Journal of Clinical Psychiatry, 68*(11), 1673-81.

Lee, L. C., Halpern, C. T., Hertz-Picciotto, I., Martin, S. L., & Suchindran, C. M. (2006). Child care and social support modify the association between maternal depressive symptoms and early childhood behaviour problems: a US national study. *Journal of Epidemiol Community Health, 60*(4), 305-10.

Levinson, D. (2006). The genetics of depression: A review. *Biological Psychiatry, 60*(2): 84-92.

Lichtenstein, P., Yip, B. H., Bjork, C., Pawitan, Y., Cannon, T. D., Sullivan P. F., & Hultman C. M. (2009). Common genetic determinants of schizophrenia and bipolar disorder in Swedish families: A population based study. *Lancet, 373*, 234-39.

Lin, C. H., Hansen, S., Wang, Z., Storm, D. R., Tapscott, S. J., & Olson, J. M. (2005). The dosage of the neuroD2 transcription factor regulates amygdala development and emotional learning. *Proceedings of the National Academy of Science of the United States of America, 102*(41), 1481–82.

Lowstuter, K. J., Sand, S., Blazer, K. R., MacDonald, D. J., Banks, K. C., Lee, C. A., Schwerin, B. U., Juarez, M., Uman, G. C., & Weitzel, J. N. (2008). Influence of genetic discrimination perceptions and knowledge on cancer genetics referral practice among clinicians. *Genetics in Medicine, 10*(9), 691–98.

Maier, W., Lichterman, D., Minges, J., Heun, R., Hallmayer, J., & Benkert, O. (1992). Schizoaffective disorder and addictive disorders with mood-incongruent psychotic features: Keep separate or combine? Evidence from a family study. *American Journal of Psychiatry, 149*, 1666–73.

Marcus, S. M. (2009). Depression during pregnancy: Rates, risks and consequences—Mother risk update 2008. *Canadian Journal of Clinical Pharmacology, 16*(1), 15–22.

Marteau, T. M., & Croyle, R. T. (1998). Psychological responses to genetic testing. *British Medical Journal, 316*, 693–96.

Mazefsky, C. A., Folstein, S. E., & Lainhart, J. E. (2008). Overrepresentation of mood and anxiety disorders in adults with autism and their first-degree relatives: What does it mean? *Autism Res, 1*(3), 193–97.

McClearn, G. E. (2004). Nature and nurture: Interaction and coaction. *American Journal of Medical Genetics, 124B*, 124–30.

Menezes, P. R., Lewis, G., Rasmussen, F, Zammit, S., Sipos, A., Harrison, G. L., Tynelius, P., & Gunnell, D. (2010). Paternal and maternal ages at conception and risk of bipolar affective disorder in their offspring. *Psychological Medicine, 40*(3), 477–85.

Meiser, B., Kasparian, N. A., Mitchell, P. B., Strong, K., Simpson, J. M., Tabassum, L., Mireskandari, S., & Schofield, P. R. (2008). Attitudes to genetic testing in families with multiple cases of bipolar disorder. *Genetic Testing, 12*(2), 233–44.

Merikangas, A. K. (1982). Assortative mating for psychiatric disorders and psychological traits. *Archives of General Psychiatry, 39*(10), 1173–80.

Merikangas, A. K., Corvin, A. P., Gallagher, L. (2009). Copy-number variants in neurodevelopmental disorders: Promises and challenges. *Trends in Genetics, 25*(12), 536–44.

Miles, J. H., McCathren, R. B., Stichter, J., Shinawi, M. Autism spectrum disorders. Accessed 2010 from *GeneReviews:* www.genereviews.org

Milne, B. J., Caspi, A., Crump, R., Poulton, R., Rutter, M., Sears, M. R., & Moffitt, T. E. (2009). The validity of the family history screen for assessing family history of mental disorders. *American Journal of Medical Genetics, 150B*, 41–49.

Mitchell, P. B., Meiser, B., Fullerton, J., & Wilhelm, K. (2010). Predictive and diagnostic genetic testing in psychiatry. *Child and Adolescent Psychiatric Clinics of North America, 33*, 225–43.

Murgatroyd, C., Patchev, A.V., Wu, Y., Micale, V., Bockmühl, Y., Fischer, D., Holsboer, F., Wotjak, C. T., Almeida, O. F., & Spengler, D., (2009). Dynamic DNA methylation programs persistent adverse effects of early-life stress. *Nature Neuroscience, 12*(12), 1559–66.

Ni, Y. G., Gold, S. J., Iredale, P. A., Terwilliger, R. Z., Duman, R. S., & Nestler, E. J. (1999). Region specific regulation of RGS4 (Regulator of G-protein-signalling protein type 4) in brain by stress and glucocorticoids: In vivo and in vitro studies. *The Journal of Neuroscience, 19*(10), 3674–80.

Owen, M. J., Craddock, N., & Jablensky, A. (2007). The genetic deconstruction of psychosis. *Schizophrenia Bulletin, 33*(4), 905–11.

Peay, H. L., Hooker, G. W., Kassem, L., & Biesecker, B. B., Family risk and related education and counseling needs: Perceptions of adults with bipolar disorder and siblings of adults with bipolar disorder. *American Journal of Medical Genetics, 149*(3), 364–71

Parry, B. L. (2009) Assessing risk and benefit: To treat or not to treat major depression during pregnancy with antidepressant medication. *American Journal of Psychiatry, 166,* 512–14.

Pedersen, C. B., & Mortensen, P. B. (2001). Evidence of a dose-response relationship between urbanicity during upbringing and schizophrenia risk. *Archives of General Psychiatry, 58,* 1039–46.

Pfeffer, N. L., Veach, P. M., & LeRoy, B. S. (2003). An investigation of genetic counselors' discussion of genetic discrimination with cancer risk patients. *Journal of Genetic Counseling, 12*(5), 419–38.

Phelan, R., Lee, L., Howe, D., & Walter, G. (2006). Parenting and mental illness: A pilot group programme for parents. *Australasian Psychiatry, 14*(4), 399–402.

Phelan, J. C., Yang, L. H., & Cruz-Rojas, R. (2006). Effects of attributing serious mental illnesses to genetic causes on orientations to treatment. *Psychiatric Services, 57,* 382–87.

Philbert, R. A., Gunter, T. D., Beach, S. R., Brody, G. H., Hollenbeck, N., Andersen, A., & Adams, W. (2009). The role of GABRA2 on risk for alcohol, nicotine, and cannabis dependence in the Iowa adoption studies. *Psychiatric Genetics, 19*(2), 91–98.

Plante, D. T., & Winkelman, J. W. (2008). Sleep disturbance in bipolar disorder: therapeutic implications. *American Journal of Psychiatry, 165*(7), 830–43.

Post, R. M. (2007). The role of BDNF in bipolar and unipolar disorder: Clinical and theoretical implications. *Journal of Psychiatry Research, 41*(12), 979–90.

Quaid, K. A., Aschen, S. R., Smiley, C. L., & Nurnberger, J. I. (2001). Perceived genetic risks for bipolar disorder in a patient population: An exploratory study. *Journal of Genetic Counseling, 10,* 41–51.

Rapoport, J. L. (2000). *Childhood onset of adult psychopathology: Clinical and research advances.* Washington, DC: American Psychiatric Publishing.

Rasmussen, S. A., & Tsuang, M. T. (1986). Clinical characteristics and family history in DSM-III obsessive-compulsive disorder. *American Journal of Psychiatry, 143,* 317–22.

Reed, S. (1975). A short history of genetic counseling. *Social Biology*, *21*, 332-39.

Reichenberg, A., Gross, R., Weiser, M., Bresnahan, M., Silverman, J., Harlap, S., Rabinowitz, J., Shulman, C., Malaspina, D., Lubin, G., Knobler, H. Y., Davidson, M., & Susser, E. (2006). Advancing paternal age and autism. *Archives of General Psychiatry*, *63*(9), 1026-32.

Resta, R., Bowles Biesecker, B., Bennett, R. L., Blum, S., Estabrooks Hahn, S., Strecker, M. N., & Williams, J. L. (2006). A new definition of genetic counseling: National Society of Genetic Counselors' task force report. *Journal of Genetic Counseling*, *15*(2), 77-83.

Resta, R. G. (2006). Defining and redefining the scope and goals of genetic counseling. *American Journal of Medical Genetics*, *142*(4), 269-75.

Ritsher, J. B., & Phelan, J. C. (2004). Internalized stigma predicts erosion of morale among psychiatric outpatients. *Psychiatry Research*, *129*, 257-65.

Schaefer, G. B., & Mendelsohn, N. J.; Professional Practice and Guidelines Committee. (2008). Clinical genetics evaluation in identifying the etiology of autism spectrum disorders. *Genetics in Medicine*, *10*(4), 301-5.

Schork, N. J., Greenwood, T. A., & Braff, D. L. (2007). Statistical genetics concepts and approaches in schizophrenia and related neuropsychiatric research. *Schizophrenia Bulletin*, *33*(1), 95-104.

Skirton, H., & Eiser, C. (2003). Discovering and addressing the client's lay construct of genetic disease: An important aspect of genetic healthcare? *Research and Theory for Nursing Practice: An International Journal*, *17*(4), 339-52.

Smoller, J. W., & Finn, C. T. (2003). Family, twin and adoption studies of bipolar disorder. *American Journal of Medical Genetics*, *123C*, 48-58.

Solari, H., Dickson, K. E., & Miller, L. (2009). Understanding and treating women with schizophrenia during pregnancy and postpartum—Motherisk Update 2008. *Canadian Journal of Clinical Pharamcology*, *16*(1), 23-32.

Spencer, T. J., Biederman, J., Wozniak, J., Faraone, S. V., Wilens, T. E., & Mick, E. (2001). Parsing pediatric bipolar disorder from its associated comorbidity with disruptive behavior disorders. *Biological Psychiatry*, *49*, 1062-70.

St-Hilaire, A., Hill, C. L., & Docherty, N. M. (2007). Coping in parents of schizophrenia patients with differing degrees of familial exposure to psychosis. *Journal of Nervous and Mental Disease*, *195*(7), 596-600.

Suto, M., Murray, G., Hle, S., Amari, E., & Michalak, E. E. (2009). What works for people with bipolar disorder? Tips from the experts. *Journal of Affective Disorders, Epub ahead of print.*

Szatmari, P., MacLean, J. E., Jones, M. B., Bryson, S. E., Zwaigenbaum, L., Bartolucci, G., Mahoney, W. J., & Tuff, L. (2000). The familial aggregation of the lesser variant in biological and nonbiological relatives of PDD probands: A family history study. *Journal of Child Psychology and Psychiatry*, *41*(5), 579-86.

Tandon, R., Keshavan, M. S., & Nasrallah, H. A. (2008). Schizophrenia: Just the facts. What we know in 2008. 2. Epidemiology and etiology. *Schizophrenia Research*, *102*(1), 1-18.

Torrey, E. F., Buka, S., Cannon,T. D., Goldstein, J. M., Seidman, L. J., Liu, T., Hadley, T., Rosso, I. M., Bearden, C., & Yolken, R. H. (2009). Paternal age as risk factor for schizophrenia: how important is it? *Schizophrenia Research*, *114*, 1-5.

Torrey, E. F., Miller, J., Rawlings, R., & Yolken, R. H. (1997). Seasonality of births in schizophrenia and bipolar disorder: A review of the literature. *Schizophrenia Research*, *28*, 1-38.

Trippitelli, C. L., Jamison, K. R., Folstein, M. F., Bartko, J. J., & DePaulo, J. R. (1998). Pilot study on patients' and spouses' attitudes toward potential genetic testing for bipolar disorder. *American Journal of Psychiatry*, *155*(7), 899-904.

Tsuang, M., Stone, W. S., & Faraone, S. V. (2001). Genes, environment and schizophrenia. *British Journal of Psychiatry*, *178*, s18-24.

Viguera, A. C., Cohen, L. S., Bouffard, S., Whitfield, T. H., & Baldessar-
ini, R. J. (2002). Reproductive decisions by women with bipolar
disorder after prepregnancy psychiatric consultation. *American
Journal of Psychiatry*, *159*(12), 2102–4.

Weil, J. (2003). Psychosocial genetic counseling in the post-nondirec-
tive era: A point of view. *Journal of Genetic Counseling*, *12*(3),
199–211.

Weissman, M. M., Wickramaratne, P., Adams, P., Wolk, S., Verdeli, H.,
& Olfson, M. (2000). Brief screening for family psychiatric history. *Archives of General Psychiatry*, *57*, 675–82.

Williams, H. J., Owen, M. J., & O'Donovan, M. C. (2009). Schizophrenia genetics: New insights from new approaches. *British Medical Bulletin*, *91*, 61–74.

Yonkers, K. A., Wisner, K. L., Steward, D. E., Oberlander, T. F., Dell,
D. L., Stotland, N., Ramin, S., Chaudron, L., & Lockwood C.
(2009). The management of depression during prehancy: A report from the American Psychiatric Association and the American College of Obstetricians and Gynecologists. *Obstetrics and
Gynecology*, *114*(3), 703–13.

Yonkers, K. A., Wisner, K. L., Stowe, K. L., Leibenluft, E., Cohen, L.,
Miller, L., Manber, R., Viguera, A., Suppes, T., & Altshuler, L.
(2004). Management of bipolar disorder during pregnancy and
the postpartum period. *American Journal of Psychiatry*, *161*,
608–20.

Yung, A. R., Phillips, L. J., Yuen, H. P., Francey, S. M., McFarlane, C. A.,
Hallgren, M., & McGorry, P. D. (2003). Psychosis prediction: 12-
month follow up of a high-risk ("prodromal") group. *Schizophrenia Research*, *60*, 21–32.

Zammit, S., Allbeck, P., Dalman, C., Lundberg, I., Hemmingson, T., &
Owen, M. J. (2003). Paternal age and risk for schizophrenia. *British Journal of Psychiatry*, *183*, 405–8.

Index

Note: Figures are noted with an *f*; tables with a *t*.